# FROM TRUST TO TAKEOVER:
## Butterworths 1938 – 1967
## A Publishing House in Transition

# FROM TRUST TO TAKEOVER
## Butterworths 1938 – 1967
## A Publishing House in Transition

by

Gordon Graham

Wildy, Simmonds & Hill Publishing

From Trust to Takeover, Butterworths 1938-1967, A Publishing
House in Transition

British Library Cataloguing-in-Publication Data:
A catalogue record for this book is available from The British
Library

ISBN 1 898029 81 4

First published in 2006 by

Wildy, Simmonds & Hill Publishing
58 Carey Street, London WC2A 2JB
England

*Dedicated to the unsung and often undervalued employees of Butterworths whose skills and devotion were its greatest assets.*

# Foreword

S TANLEY BOND, who owned and ran Butterworths, England's leading law publisher, from 1895 to 1943, was a giant among publishers. He was a visionary endowed with great courage who also built the financial resources to match his vision. He introduced multi-volume encyclopaedias into law publishing. The greatest of these was *Halsbury's Laws of England,* which first began to appear in 1907. *Halsbury* was not only the greatest of the encyclopaedias, it also carried the greatest financial risk. It took a long time to get established - in Stanley Bond's own words `I went to bed facing blue ruin, but woke up a comparatively wealthy man'. The story of Bond's successes is ably told in H. Kay Jones's *Butterworths: History of a Publishing House* (1980), brought up to date in a second edition by the author of this book in 1997.

Bond made very few mistakes in his publishing career, as those books make clear; but like a hero in Greek tragedy, there was one chink in his armour. Whether because he was too focused on his business, or because he too much enjoyed being the eligible and wealthy bachelor, or simply out of *hubris,* he left it too late to get married - too late, that is, to father children who could take over the business after his death. When he died, aged 65, in 1943, his two sons were mere aged three and one. Shortly before he died, Bond set up a system of management by trustees in the hope that they would keep the business in good order until his elder son Ian was able to take over. As in many great tragedies, this plan came to within an inch of success. By the time the trustees sold Butterworths to the International Publishing Corporation (I.P.C.) in 1967, Ian was aged 27 had already acquired experience in publishing management and was ready to enter his patrimony. So what went wrong? This book sets out to unravel the mystery.

By a strange quirk of fate, the author, Gordon Graham, employed Ian Bond in 1965/66 without knowing his connection with Butterworths. He also met many of the other participants in the drama, including the one man who, above all, was responsible for thwarting Stanley Bond's plans: his Nemesis. The reader of this lively and well-written book - part business history, part human drama - will meet that man in these pages as he is first brought into the business, then sets about turning it on its head, and then engineers its sale.

Neville Cusworth

(Chairman of Butterworths 1990-9)

# *Author's Preface*

AFTER joining Butterworths, England's premier law publisher, in 1974, I became interested in the company's history. It had been founded in 1818. How had it achieved its eminence? Kay Jones, who had retired as Deputy Managing Director after forty years of service, undertook prodigious research in the company's archives and among his ex-colleagues. The result was *Butterworths: History of a Publishing House*, published in 1980. A revised and updated edition was published in 1997. It is a comprehensive professional history with descriptions of products and people and places; appointments and tenure; anecdotes; meetings; finances – a definitive work.

Butterworths' history falls into four parts – the 19th century when it was sedately and modestly run by the original Butterworths; the first four decades of the 20th century when it was dynamically built into England's and the Empire's leading law publisher by Stanley Bond, whose father had purchased the company in 1895; the next 25 years when it was owned by the Bond family trust; and the last quarter of the twentieth century when it was a division of the International Publishing Corporation, which became Reed International and latterly Reed-Elsevier, who remain the owners today.

This book is about the third of these four periods. It describes the prolonged three-way power struggle between the Bond family, the trustees of Bond's will and the managers. The story is in some ways a morality tale and in others a case study of the perils and pitfalls of family ownership after the founder of a company dies.

There are very few books on the influence of personalities on a company's governance. Family-owned companies are secretive and the publicly owned corporations who take them over are not interested in history. Such books are best written in retrospect, but not too long in retrospect because the best insights into complex relationships are gained by interviewing those who participated. I was fortunate to meet a few of those who played parts in Butterworths from the 1930's onwards.

The strength of feelings of those who have devoted their professional lives to an institution should never be under-estimated. Kay Jones's 1980 book, in which he conscientiously tried to avoid giving offence, drew the ire of some of his ex-colleagues whose memories differed from his. Kay reached the point when he could no longer bear to read some of the letters he received and passed them to me unopened. These surviving employees were often the only sources of information because so much of the drama took place behind closed doors. Sensitive documents seldom reached the archive. One key player directed, after he was ousted, that all his files be burned. Kay's history was written while Stanley Bond's widow was still alive and for this reason steered clear of the emotional strains within the family, involving mainly her second husband and her son Ian.

I have had access to all the business correspondence that survived. The challenge to the historian in reading business letters is to divine the emotions behind the careful phrasing. Inevitably, the letters from and to the people who form this story were written by executives or senior managers. The unsung heroes who sustained the company through its travails were the rank-and-file employees who bestowed their labour and loyalty on an institution which they idealized, but left no written record. I was able to interview one or two of them.

There would be no point in writing this story unless it had contemporary and future relevance. Its main lesson, which I (like many others) have learned in sixty years of management experience – in the army, in family businesses and in two of the world's leading publishing corporations – is that management succeeds best when animosity and crony-ism are kept to a minimum.

# CONTENTS

## CHAPTER ONE

## *The Trust*

THE *Daily Telegraph* of 29th September 1943 reported that the estate of Stanley Shaw Bond, who had died in February of that year, amounted to half a million pounds. The sum was seen as "surprisingly large". The report described Bond as "a tall, shy figure who masked behind a languid manner great business ability". It was his drive and initiative that had "caused Butterworths to branch out all over the dominions and America. He probably gave more employment to the junior bar of Britain and the dominions than all the firms of solicitors there put together".

*The Church Times*, in an obituary of 17th February 1943, had described Bond as "a debonair and soigné figure who was never without a flower in his bottonhole and smiles came quickly to his lips". *The Aberdeen Evening Express* of the same date referred to Bond's house parties as "among the highlights of the season". They called him "first and foremost an open air man. Shooting, stalking, fishing and golf were the very breath of life to him". *The Times*, of 16th February, referred to Bond as "Vice-Chairman of the Central Board of Finance of the Church of England and Chairman of the Financial Commission of the Church Assembly" before mentioning that he had been Chairman of Butterworths. However, at the meeting of the Church's Board of Finance on the following day, Earl Grey praised Bond's publishing achievements. "Butterworths," he said, "was co-extensive with the British Empire. Since the Roman Empire, the only person besides Mr Bond to attempt to codify the system of law had been Napoleon".

None of the obituaries paid Stanley Bond the tribute that the subsequent history of Butterworths made clear: he was one of the outstanding British publishers of the twentieth century. Working in the unglamorous field of law publishing, he was not known in the book trade and did not wish to be. He was as innovative as Allen Lane and as professional as Stanley Unwin (both of whom were knighted for their services to publishing and were the subjects of numerous biographies.)

His publishing career, from 1895 to 1943, anticipated developments that were not recognized until the '60s and '70s, when the accumulation of information began to overtake the power of the printed word to transmit it. Bond originated the multi-volume professional encyclopedia, with supplements and up-dates, which was the precursor of the electronic database. Told that it was impossible to codify the laws of England; he went ahead and did it, after pursuing the Lord Halsbury to his holiday hotel on the Riviera to get his imprimatur. In Bond's own words:

> I decided I must have the support of the top men if the idea was to succeed. I determined to invite the Lord Chancellor to be Editor in Chief and I obtained an interview with him. He was obviously interested but said he must have time to think it over. I waited for a while and then hearing nothing, I made enquiries to find, to my consternation, that Lord Halsbury had gone on holiday to Nice. As I needed to start as soon as possible, I took myself to Nice and finally ran Lord Halsbury to earth in an hotel.

> I accosted him in the foyer and in surprised tones he said, "Hello Bond, what are you doing here?" I replied, "I've come for my answer, my Lord." "But I'm on holiday," Halsbury replied. "I'm sorry, my Lord," I said, "but I must have a reply one way or the other." "Well, Bond," he said, "I admire you for your cheek … and, yes, I'll do it. Only, Bond, the labourer is worthy of his hire … eh?" "Name your fee, my Lord," I replied. He named it and it was a stiff one. I pulled out my cheque book and wrote him a cheque for the lot. "Done, my Lord," I said.

Bond started *Halsbury's Laws of England* in 1907 and completed it, in twenty-eight volumes, in 1917. The keys to good publishing, then, as now, were innovation, vision, determination,

2

concentration and readiness to take risks. After completion of the work, Bond said that he was close to bankruptcy, but woke up the next morning as a rich man.

Bond had started in the business humbly. Butterworths had been purchased in 1895 by his father, who owned a competing company called Shaw & Sons. Bond was then a troublesome eighteen-year-old, and his father hoped that working in this tiny company (which had been purchased for £5,500 when the last Butterworth died) would keep his son quiet. Little did he know. Thirty years later Stanley Bond had made his fortune and his name, and had won his way into the establishment of the rich and exclusive. He divided his time between a West End flat in London and an estate near Chichester. Every summer he rented a grand house in the Scottish Highlands. His favourite was Braemar Castle. His house parties there were legendary, with guests selected from the gentry.

The Scottish connection was important to Stanley Bond. He liked to appear in a kilt. At first the resident Scots regarded him with reserve, but he won them over with his style and generosity, and anyway didn't care very much what they thought. The proximity of Bond's summer rentals to the royal family's home at Balmoral undoubtedly appealed to Bond who, according to Barry Rose, editor for fifty years of Bond's favourite journal *Justice of the Peace*, had the same physician as King George V. Bond's reverence for royalty is evident in a photograph, taken at Braemar, where he is seen receiving from Her Majesty Queen Mary a painting by Winston Churchill, which he had bought at a charity auction.

Marjorie Bond, a niece of Stanley born in 1910, recalls "Uncle Stanley's" visits to her childhood home. She remembers him as "very kind, generous and thoughtful". One Christmas, she recalls, he asked the local vicar for a list of the neediest families in the village and had himself and Marjorie driven to their houses, where he distributed blankets and other comforts.

Bond was religious and never missed Sunday service. Among his good works, Marjorie recalls, was a charity for the deaf and dumb, in which the then Duke of York, who was to become King George VI, was also interested. Marjorie Bond confirms that her uncle did enjoy high society. She remembers one party at Braemar Castle attended by the King and Queen, which featured a twilight procession and a dance called the "Paul Jones" involving a constant change of partners, in which the Royals participated.

Sir Peter Smithers, who was to become a distinguished diplomat and politician and also was a key player in the drama of the Bond succession, has vivid memories of life in Bond's Scottish Highland retreats in the '20s and '30s. Sir Peter's father, who was a country gentleman, had met Bond in the south of France, and passed the test as a worthy participant in the summer parties. Smithers remembers Bond as "in some ways a very sociable man and in other ways unapproachable". When in Scotland, he liked to have people around him, but did not allow this to interfere with his daily communication with his office in Bell Yard, adjacent to the Royal Courts of Justice in London. Some of the guests became good friends. Others, according to Sir Peter, were there for what they could get. Bond apparently ruled his house parties with a firm hand. One lady who displeased him found on her breakfast tray a note saying: "The car will be at the door at 10.30 to take you to the train at Ballater".

By the 1930's, Bond was very rich. Braemar Castle was the most distinguished rental on Deeside. He had two Rolls Royces, driven by a wild chauffeur called Fraser, who habitually had two Sealyhams lashed to his wrist while he drove, a custom which caused some apprehension to passengers. Bond also had "a wonderful butler called Cloughessie who served him hand and foot".

Braemar Castle was his summer home, to which Bond moved his ménage from West Dean, his country estate in Sussex, where his lifestyle had all the idiosyncrasies and appurtenances of the landed gentry. Marjorie Bond recalls that there was a sedan chair in the hall on which one morning she found Earl Grey reading the *Sunday Times*. West Dean had its own golf course. Bond also found time to participate in the social circuit at places like Nice and Biarritz, where he was accompanied by his sister Mary.

Until the age of sixty, Bond was a bachelor. In fact, in that year he was Chairman of the Bachelors' Club, so his marriage to the thirty-year-old Myrtle Fletcher took everyone by surprise, except his niece Marjorie Bond. Stanley had taken her with him on a skiing holiday in Arosa in the winter of 1937. After a week, Stanley said he had to leave his niece alone, but he would call her, which he did a week later from nearby Klosters, where he was holidaying with Myrtle.

Myrtle Fletcher had frequently accompanied her parents, Lt Colonel A F Fletcher and Lady Theresa Fletcher (sister of the Seventh Earl Fitzwilliam) when they were houseguests at Braemar. Under the heading "Bachelors Think Her Ideal: Chairman is forgiven" *The Evening Star* reported:

5

No make-up, perfectly natural, and a great country lover. That is the girl who has captured the heart of Mr Stanley S Bond, the chairman of the Bachelors' Club.

Indeed, Miss Violet Myrtle Fletcher, eldest daughter of Lieut.-Col. Alan Fletcher, of the 17th Lancers, and Lady Theresa Fletcher of Arundel, Sussex, has taken the Bachelors' Club by storm.

Nearly all of them are attending the wedding at St Mary Abbot's, Kensington, on Thursday.

Moreover, they have privately passed a resolution that Miss Fletcher is the only type of womanhood who is a worthy excuse for waiving the rules.

Here are the attributes these bachelors applaud:

She uses no lip-stick.

She has no fussy feminine mannerisms

She is liked by everyone, and was a favourite of the late Earl Haig – her Godfather.

Although not strikingly pretty, she has enormous charm.

Because she fulfills all these conditions, Miss Fletcher has saved her fiancée a two-guinea fine. It is understood that his fellow-members have decided to pay it.

When a "Star" reporter asked her how she felt breaking up the Bachelors' Club, she laughed gaily – and revealed a secret.

"At least a third of the members are married," she declared. "If they barred married men the club couldn't exist."

"Mr Bond will probably continue as chairman, in fact, and I shall encourage him."

She is fair-haired, grey-eyed, and, according to the bachelors, can face a rainstorm or cloud burst and still retain her attraction, equanimity – and dimples.

"I am 30," she said, "but my fiance is considerably older. I am not allowed to tell you his exact age."

Marriage brought the new Mrs Bond into a world that she little understood. It is believed by those who were in Butterworths at that time that Stanley Bond married in order to become a father. In two years, Myrtle Bond gave birth to two sons, whom Bond saw not only as the heirs to his estate but as the future managers of his business. To this end he established a complex trust in his will, to which he attached specific instructions about his sons' future.

The business was to be preserved so that they would be able to take it over. In a letter dated 7th May 1942, written from Braemar Castle, he expressed his "wishes and requests" to the trustees of his will. The letter concerns his elder son Ian, but he noted that the same wishes should apply to his younger son Brian:

1.　He shall be brought up in the Church of England and specially helped and influenced to follow the Christian Faith.

2.　His name is down for Eton: as regards a prep school, it will probably be wise to ask the advice of the House Master at Eton.

3.　From Eton, I hope he will go to Oxford and take a Law Degree, which will be helpful to him in the business.

4.　From Oxford, I hope greatly he will go to Butterworths, to be trained for [that] publishing work. He should go through each department. Sometimes, young men have ideas that they would like to do this, that or the other thing; but I do not think he should lightly turn aside from his father's work. Rather he should look upon it as a duty to look after his mother's interest in the business, and subsequently his own.

5.　I express the hope that he will not associate himself with London life, apart from his business connection with the same; but rather have his interests, outside business, in country life.

6.    I hope he may be elected a member of the Carlton Club and a University Club in London and not the Bachelors' Club.

Stanley Bond's final will, dated 10th September 1942, is a twenty-five-page printed document, drawn up by his solicitors, Bull and Bull.  It sets up a trust, of which the trustees were to be Gilbert West, senior partner of Bull and Bull (with Douglas Niekirk as alternate); Guy Hanmer, an army officer; Kenneth Moore, a prominent City figure and Bond's principal financial adviser, and Bond's protégé Peter Smithers, who was then on war service with the navy. Mrs Bond, as the principal legatee, was empowered to appoint additional trustees. In the event, the only one she appointed was herself. Hanmer was soon to resign, and West handed over to Niekirk.

Before stating the terms of the trust, Bond directed an immediate cash payment of £2,000 to Mrs Bond, plus all his personal chattels, "except my collections of drawings by French, Italian and Dutch Masters and such other personal chattels as are specifically bequeathed ...". The will also asked Mrs Bond to pass the grandfather clock and oak writing cabinet, which Bond had inherited from his father, respectively to their sons Ian and Brian.

The trustees were required to pay three-quarters of the income from the estate to Mrs Bond, and to hold the balance of the income in trust for Ian and Brian, until they attained the age of twenty-five - which would be 29th December 1965 in the case of Ian. The will sought to ensure the continuity of Butterworths – "a company of an exceptional nature requiring special qualifications in the persons who have the management thereof". The trustees were directed to invite Moore, West (or Niekirk) and three of the senior managers, John Whitlock, E C Leader and Lawrence Jones to serve as directors. The fees payable to directors were to be "at an annual rate and not dependent on attendance at board meetings". They were not "to exceed in the aggregate £500 per annum to any individual director", with the exceptions of the chairman and deputy chairman who were to receive £1,500 and £750 respectively.

A codicil specified individual legacies - elk horns, a bracket clock and a bronze statue of Napoleon to Mrs Bond; family silver to Bond's brother Frank; a gold watch with platinum chain, platinum and amethyst cufflinks, gold diamond cufflinks, a gold matchbox, a pair of shot guns, a Mauser rifle, a prayer book and a Bible to his son Ian; a Lancaster gun, a Mannlicher rifle, a platinum wristwatch, a sporting silver wristwatch, platinum and diamond cufflinks, and black onyx and diamond cufflinks and buttons to his son Brian; and another Mauser rifle to Bond's nephew Kenneth, son of his brother Frank. Distant relatives and godchildren were left legacies of £50 or £100. The bailiff of Bond's estate and his chauffeur were left annuities of £130 per annum. Long-service employees were awarded small legacies.

The codicil also bequeathed shares in Butterworths to the trustees and directors: 500 to Moore; 250 each to Hanmer and Smithers; and 250 to West or Niekirk, whichever one of them would have proved the will. Whitlock, Leader and Jones received 750 shares each. Seabrook Emery the company secretary got 500, and Helen Osborn, Bond's secretary since 1938, 100. Only the trustees were to get their shares immediately. The others were to be held by the trustees for five years, during which the beneficiaries would receive the dividends. Those who were still employed five years after Bond's death would receive their shares absolutely. If any of the legatees wanted to sell their shares, they were required to offer them in the first place to the trustees. Bond expressed "a strong hope" that Helen Osborn would continue to be employed.

Bond's instructions to his trustees required them to look after Mrs Bond and to keep the company intact until the sons were twenty-five years old. Since the elder son was only two when Bond died, the trustees had a formidable task.

## CHAPTER TWO

## *The Bond Empire*

IN order to understand what happened to Butterworths after Stanley Bond's death, it is necessary to know something of what the company was like in the few years before his death. Butterworths was Bond's creation, and he ran it autocratically. By the 1930s, it was a dominant force in law publishing in England. The great multi-volume works (*Encyclopedia of Forms and Precedents, Halsbury's Laws of England, English and Empire Digest, Halsbury's Statutes, Atkin's Court Forms*) were the bedrock of the company. Bond had founded branches in India (1910), Australia (1911), Canada (1912), New Zealand (1914) and South Africa (1934). In the late 1930s Bond began to diversify from law into medicine, with the publication of *The British Encyclopaedia of Medical Practice.*

All the companies were tightly controlled. Bond required daily financial reports from overseas. The people who ran these companies were dispatched from England as colonial overseers.

*Justice of the Peace* (JP) a journal for magistrates, was a Butterworth publication about which Stanley Bond was sentimental, perhaps because he was working on it in Shaw and Sons, his father's company, when he entered Butterworths in 1895. Barry Rose, who was still the Editor in 1993, and had been the owner of "The World's Oldest Law Journal" since 1969, joined Butterworths in 1941 and found himself unexpectedly Editor and Manager of JP in 1943 at the age of twenty. After Bond's death, Mrs Bond told Rose that Bond had regarded JP as "Butterworths in miniature". It exemplifies the personal publishing formula that Bond developed: accurate and up-to-date professional information for a discrete constituency which buys automatically, repeatedly, directly from the publisher - and pays in advance. In his will, Bond kept JP separate from Butterworths. It was inherited personally by Mrs Bond, to whom Rose was directly responsible. Rose recalls Mrs Bond bringing her son,

11

Ian, then aged eleven, to visit him, and discussing the idea that Ian might start his career by working on JP.

Rose characterized Bond's management style as idiosyncratic even by the standards of the 1930s. For example, as in many offices in those days, the "office boy" was indispensable. Bond required that there should always be a boy sitting outside his office, listening for the bell. When the boy entered in response to the bell, no words were exchanged. One ring meant that the cigarette case needed to be filled. Two rings meant that the fire had to be made up. Three rings required the boy to go into the adjoining lavatory and pull the chain.

One of Bond's confidants - a man called Cooper who had the reputation of being Bond's office spy – recalled a game that he and Bond played on the occasions when he accompanied Bond to Euston Station, to catch the night train to Scotland. Bond had the habit of borrowing Cooper's newspaper and departing with it. Cooper tried, not always successfully, to delay purchasing his paper until Bond had gone. "Of course", Cooper conceded, "one has to be fair. At Christmas Mr Bond would always give a pound to the newspaper seller at the bottom of Bell Yard".

Seabrook Emery liked to tell the story of his summer vacation in 1933. He had obtained permission from Bond to be away for the first two weeks in August, and had booked a holiday for himself and his wife in the south of France. Permission was given, and every now and then Emery reminded Bond that he would be away for these weeks. On the Friday before his departure, he went to bid Bond farewell. "Oh yes", said Bond, "where are you going?" "To the south of France," Emery replied. "Oh, I can't have a member of my senior staff leaving for the continent." "But sir, we have already booked." "You must cancel it." Emery and his wife went to Margate.

When Stanley Bond was not in Scotland, he was either at his London flat at 7 Cleveland Row, opposite St James's Palace, or, from the mid-1930s, at his country estate, West Dean Park near

Chichester. At none of his residences did he have time for politics, but at all of them he did have time for church. He never missed Sunday service. Nor did his guests, whatever their religious habits. Simon Partridge, who was hired by Bond in 1942 and was to become Managing Director of the UK law company in 1975, got his job in 1940 because his father, a bishop, had served with Bond on the Central Board of Finance of the Church of England. In the Butterworth house journal forty years later, Partridge recalled his job interview with Bond:

> When I got there he received me kindly. 'We're going to share lunch together' he boomed and my spirits rose. They sank again when I saw it was meant literally. He had a plate of steamed fish and soggy vegetables in front of him. Half of this he shovelled onto a spare plate. He did the same with the rhubarb and custard. 'Wade in, my boy,' he said jovially. 'I'm glad to share my lunch with you as they always give me too much.' I looked at the portions thoughtfully. They seemed far from large when divided in half. I consoled myself with the thought that at least I had a glass of water all to myself.
>
> During the frugal repast Stanley asked me how I'd got on with Emery and what I wanted to do. 'I must earn some money so as to help my mother,' I said. 'What do you advise?' He started as though stung by a wasp. 'Money,' he said, 'you'd better go into munitions.' At intervals thereafter he snorted indignantly and murmured 'money' to himself. I'd obviously said the wrong thing.
>
> After lunch I returned to Emery. He asked how I'd got on. 'Mr Bond says I ought to go into munitions,' I said, 'but I can't say it appeals.' 'No,' said Emery shaking with suppressed mirth. 'Well I think the idea is for you to come here for a trial. I'll write to you about it.' This was news to me. I didn't know what the firm did, let alone its name.

In due course the letter came. It offered me three months' trial at £200 pa. The letter seemed less than optimistic as to my chances of success.

Thirteen years later I got a letter from Helen Osborn, the company secretary. 'The Board have noted,' she said, 'that you are still on three months' trial and they have instructed me to offer you a permanent position.' I heaved a sigh of relief. It had been an anxious time.

Bond was a man of paradoxes. Meanness alongside generosity; autocracy alongside humility; shrewd business sense alongside humanity. Peter Smithers recalls an instance of the kindness that Bond was capable of extending. When Smithers, in his upper teens, showed interest in attending his first London society ball at Dorchester House, Bond sent him to his own tailor in Savile Row to buy a tailcoat on his account. He also provided a suitable girl.

An unpublished obituary, submitted to *The Times*, relates that once, in Scotland, Bond, "hearing a young officer on leave from abroad had enjoyed miserable sport during his stay at the local inn", arranged that "the stranger should spend the day fishing his best stretch of water and with the keenest ghillie".

Bond's remoteness from day-to-day contact with employees below senior rank occasionally made him gullible. One employee tried to take advantage of Bond's religious observance by attending a Saints' Day Service in the church of West Dean. Bond and the apple-polishing employee, whom the senior managers had been keeping well clear of Bond because they suspected his motives, were the only people in the congregation. After walking back to the house with the employee, Bond complimented John Whitlock on the man's sterling calibre. Bond died before the employee could take advantage of the good impression he had made, which was just as well, as he subsequently went to prison for seven years for fraud against the Law Society.

Until 1938, there was one Butterworth senior executive who towered above the others and who felt entitled to regard himself as the heir to the throne. George Bellew had been hired in 1906. Like all Bond employees, he was required to sign a legal document requiring him "while he shall continue in the service of Messieurs Butterworth and Company, faithfully and diligently to serve them ... and at all times obey and comply with lawful commands and directions in relation to the said business, and to the utmost of his skill and ability serve and promote the interests of Messieurs Butterworth and Company". The Memorandum also required that employees should not divulge or disclose "any of the secrets, concerns or affairs of their employers". In the event of their leaving the company, for whatever reason, they were forbidden to engage in law publishing or bookselling for five years. Bellew's copperplate letter of application is dated 22nd February 1906. It enclosed a reference from the Literary Director of Sir Isaac Pitman and Son, certifying that Bellow has been "my personal clerk and has served me faithfully and well and has grown - not merely in inches - but in intellectual sense since he came to use in the autumn of 1904". After detailing his experience with Pitman, Bellew wrote: "I may say that I am well educated, have a good knowledge of literature and feel I could do good work for you. The salary I require is about £2 per week". He concluded his letter with a statement that he was not afraid of work. Bond annotated the letter in pencil: "fairly good and would suit by and by no doubt".

Bellew suited for thirty-two years. Kay Jones sums up Bellew's career as follows:

George Bellew was the key man between the wars. General Manager in 1910, he became the first Managing Director when Bond's UK business was turned into a company in 1927. There is a tendency to belittle his contribution to the development of the company, for the reasons that he was overshadowed by Stanley Bond; that he was feared rather than loved; and that he was removed from office in 1938, at the comparatively young age of fifty-one. Yet Bond relied on Bellew, as his second-in-command for nearly thirty years.

Inspiration came from Bond; his was the creative genius. Bellew was the administrator and the salesman.

It appears that he set out to make himself feared in his daily dealings with the staff, whereas Bond from his more Olympian height was able to afford benevolence. Such kindnesses on Bellew's part as are remembered seem to have been designed to modify a decision of Bond's. Bellew tended to talk in riddles, with the result that he did not get the best out of his staff ...

Those who delighted in intrigue had ample opportunity for playing Bond and Bellew off against each other, but the excellence of the product and the hard core of conscientious workers made Butterworths proof against the effects of this. It was rumoured that Bellew kept a revolver in his desk. Certainly he had on his desk, not only a switch to light the 'engaged' sign over the door, but a switch to lock the door, which could be a very frightening ploy. Bond was liked and respected; Bellew was disliked and feared. Bond used him as a watch-dog, but the watch-dog (through his secretary) also watched his master. A member of staff who had been seen by Bond could expect to be questioned by Bellew's secretary.

George Bellew

Bellew's downfall was precipitated by John Whitlock, Publishing Manager, who had joined Butterworths in 1923, and the accountant, E C Leader, whom Bond had hired in 1931 to be his top financial man. Barney Barns, who ran Butterworths in South Africa from 1949 to 1975, remembers the bitter animosity between Leader and Bellew which, he says, Bond encouraged. In any publishing house there is a natural tension between accounts, sales and publishing. A year after Whitlock and Leader had been added to the Board, on which Bellew had previously been the sole executive member (apart from Bond) Bellew assembled the staff to make a dramatic speech of resignation from the top of the circular staircase in the Bell Yard office. Barns recalls that Leader stationed himself in a strategic passageway, from which he could observe without being observed, and, fearing physical assault by Bellew, asked Barns to arrange that the male members of the accounts staff should form a defensive ring around him. Thus Bellew and Leader presaged a long period of mistrust and bickering among managers, not suppressed by Bond while he was alive, and a serious cancer in the management after his death.

Bond let Bellew go without any evidence of regret. Marjorie Bond feels that Bellew's downfall was connected with Bond's marriage. She recalls that Bellew had offended Bond by referring publicly, in a speech about a trip that he and Bond had made to India together, to the Indians' surprise that Bond was not married. The remaining years of Bellew's life were attended by petty litigation and sustained animosity. He died penniless in 1955, leaving his non-existent estate to a Miss Gardiner, who had been his secretary while he was in Butterworths and his housekeeper after he resigned and had pre-deceased him by a few months. Butterworths paid his debts - through the intervention of Emery, who had been a silent witness of Bellew's downfall in 1938. Bellew's file reveals that he had been living on a pension of £100 a month, from which income tax at ten shillings in the pound was deducted before payment. A year after Bellew's resignation and before he was paid £3,800 in lieu of six months' notice. Douglas Niekirk, of the solicitors Bull and Bull, who was later to join the Butterworth Board, wrote to Bond enclosing keys that Bellew had handed over to him in return for his pension agreement. Bellew, he reported, "did not raise any question this morning about the chair supposed to have been taken away by Mr Leader". Bond annotated the letter laconically in side notes to Emery: "Deal with"; "Watch"; and (with regard to the chair) "Forget".

Bond's marriage to Myrtle Fletcher took place three weeks after Bellew's resignation. On 1 November 1938, the day after Bellew resigned, Bond wrote to Lawrence Jones, who was running Butterworths in Australia, inviting him to return to the UK and become the company's Sales Director. "If you wish to remain in Australia," he wrote, "I do not think your supervision of India from Sydney would be much help to me. Supervision of India, such as is very badly required, must be done in London by someone in daily personal touch with me and the board of directors". Bond's letter also comments at length on the Munich crisis. After informing Jones that "plans for rearmament and for the manufacture of aero planes are being pressed forward with incredible speed" he declared himself "optimistic for the future peace of Europe". Bond confided in Jones that he was pursuing the relative merits of sinking capital in local publishing in South Africa or India as against major new publications in London. He pronounced the *British Encyclopedia of Medical Practice* "an outstanding success; in India alone we have nearly a thousand subscribers".

In his haste, Bond had failed to inform the other directors of his intentions for Lawrence Jones. Jones had accepted and told all his friends when a postscript arrived that the appointment was subject to board approval.

Jones agreed to come back to the UK with high expectations, which however he had grounds to modify even before his arrival. In a five-page letter, dated 7 December 1938 Bond outlined what Jones's duties would be: "I agree that, unless there is some pressing need for your presence in London on Saturday mornings, you need not take the journey just for the Saturday mornings; but the heads of the departments under your control should report to you by telephone and the weekend is a very good time to read over papers and drafts, if you find yourself in arrears; with the exception that there must be a Director on duty at Bell Yard every Saturday, a roster must be made, and you must take your turn in the roster". He went on to veto Jones's proposal that he make a stay in Canada before returning to the UK from Australia, but authorized a stopover at the Toronto office, pointing out that he could "get a through train from Vancouver to Toronto, and there by arrangement could spend three or four days with Mr Elliott and the two travellers ... with a view to getting in touch with them and forming an opinion of their capacity and absorbing their general knowledge. This must be limited to three or four days. It would take me only three days to lap up the whole position in Canada and I have no doubt that you would be as quick". Bond finished the letter by turning down Jones's suggestion about a pension. "Your suggested idea of a pension fund does not commend itself to me ... I should prefer to deal with individual cases as I have done in the past".

Bond was more at home with external advisers than with his managers. His most trusted confidants were Gilbert West, senior partner of his solicitors, Bull and Bull, and Kenneth Moore who had been a director since 1937 and who, although not personally close, was greatly respected by Bond. A letter from Bond to Moore dated 29 March 1942 suggested that he and Moore should have lunch at Hoares, who were Bond's bankers. "I venture to hope that it would not bore you too much to have lunch with them; they have a most admirable lunch, and make it a practice to invite clients whom they consider important, and I think I can guarantee your having some pre-war sherry".

Bond not being one for casual chats or cosy conversations, Lawrence Jones wrote him long letters several times a week. On 29 July 1942, he wrote: "I have noticed in recent months that whenever any question in connection with Miss Rich has come up for discussion you have expressed yourself as opposed to her promotion and even to her retention. You have, of course, never seen Miss Rich and therefore it is my duty to make it clear to you what type of worker she is because I know that you would not wish to be unfair to her. She has had a better education than most juniors that we get in this office. She has the misfortune to be a Jewess and she escaped from German Poland just before the War.

That in itself is not against her in my opinion and it prevents her being called up so that in some ways it is an advantage". Jones had apparently had his knuckles rapped by Bond over the firing of an unsatisfactory clerk without obtaining Bond's permission. He was getting his own back.

During one month (July 1942), Jones's memos to Bond comprised sixty-three closely typed pages. Bond's replies (typed with a red ribbon) covered thirteen pages.

One of Bond's letters was a handwritten note from the Royal Northern Club, Aberdeen, headed "Clark Hall", which was a new publication about juvenile courts. The note read: "There are four women who are called 'distinguished women' by the Aberdeen Press and Journal. I think you should see some of them for a testimonial re Clark, the line to be efficient handling of children's courts: Barbara Ward, Letitia Fairfield, Dorothy Sayers and Margaret Bondfield. Consider please and possibly it would be worth getting Mr Whitlock to let us have some advance copies. If Letitia does not want to, I am sure Dorothy would!! SSB'.

Jones was generally seeking more authority, and Bond was generally telling him why he couldn't have it. The agenda for one of their weekly meetings consisted of thirty-two items. Under "Australia" the topic was "Mrs Robertson - £6 today - £6.10s proposed". Item 4(c), under New Zealand, was "Earthquake".

The Jones/Bond correspondence reveals that Bond had plans and ideas beyond both legal and medical publishing. This is confirmed by Sir Alex Cairncross, who was then an economics lecturer in Glasgow University, of which he was to become Chancellor in the 1980s. In 1942 he was about to write, although he could not know it then, one of the great classic textbooks on economics. Lawrence Jones referred to this book in a letter to Bond dated 13 April 1942 under a paragraph headed "Your Book on Economics by Mr Cairncross", and expressed himself as doubtful about the commitment. Bond was here demonstrating his instinct for opportunism. Cairncross had been recommended to take his manuscript to Thornton Butterworth, the publishers of the Home University Library and wrote to Butterworths by mistake. So Bond, who had never published an economics textbook, seized upon it eagerly. "I was told," says Cairncross, "that Bond wanted to turn his firm into the British McGraw-Hill". Caincross's book became a great asset in Butterworths' list.

Bond's vision was always restless. By the 1930s he felt he had established Butterworths in a position of such pre-eminence with the legal profession that becoming a Butterworth author was seen as an aid to professional advancement. Sir William Dale, who signed his first contract with Butterworths in 1932, and his last one in 1985, recalled in 1992 that Lord Atkin "offered to put me in touch with Butterworths". When he wrote his second book, he naturally submitted it to Butterworths.

One of the sources of Butterworths' strength was that Bond, although he had established a company which was editorially driven, attached great importance to sales and especially to the training of salesmen. He understood from the outset the need to know customers, to meet them and to sell them a product which would bring repeat business. He wrote to Lawrence Jones on 21 May 1942: "Our policy is to build up sound properties. There is not really very much advantage in selling one particular book for which there may not be a future edition and which leads nowhere". After citing several publications with serial qualities, Bond said in his letter to Jones: "I want you to reflect on these remarks of mine and let me have your reaction". In a handwritten PS he added "Please consider this note carefully and write me next week on this line of thought". Bond obviously thought highly of Jones, but was careful not to give him a free rein and was sparing with his compliments. He did not want another Bellew. In the same letter he said that building the *Law Journal* "must come under the fire of your fierce energy after the War".

On 2 January 1942, one item in a five-page memo from Jones concerned "Staff in Calcutta". Jones said that he was satisfied "that the editorial staff is being kept down to the minimum and the particulars of this I have always before me. As regards the number of *peons* [messengers] employed and the packers and go-down [warehouse] staff I do not see how anyone from here can usefully interfere. Both the men we have in India have adequate experience of Indian questions to deal with a matter of this sort which surely is one that can be handled by the Managers on the spot".

There was little democracy around Stanley Bond. He regarded himself as a patriarch, while he was in fact an autocrat. It never occurred to him that his company should have a pension plan. "I look after my people", he said. Kay Jones, on opening a package of books sent to his home, found an anonymous view of Butterworths' reputation as paymaster. The packer had written on the wrapping paper: "The wages of sin is death, but the wages of Butterworth are worse".

Bond could write just as bluntly as the packer. He wrote to one manager "If you have nerves you should cut out all forms of alcohol from beer upwards and should have the guts to do it absolutely ... If (Butterworths) was a public company and I was Chairman, I think it is very doubtful that I should consider I was justified in retaining your services ...".

In May 1942 Bond wrote from Braemar Castle to an employee who had been on sick leave and was claiming that salesmen were treated better than he was. He advised the employee to take a complete rest "during the next two or three months", making no mention of the fact that staff who went sick were paid full salary only for the first month and then half-pay for a further three months. With regard to the man's complaint of discrimination, Bond wrote: "The Company looks upon representatives and office staff (professional or otherwise) as being in two entirely separate categories. A representative aged twenty-five may earn £500 per year if he is a good man. An office man, on the other hand, may also be a good go-ahead fellow but of a different temperament. At twenty-five he will be earning say £300 per year and he is entitled to look forward to earning £500 a year at thirty-five. By the time both representative and office man are fifty years of age they have earned the same amount of £sd during the course of their business careers, but one chose the precarious, more exciting kind of life, with the rewards coming earlier, while the other took up a duller but safer career". He concluded by saying: "Get yourself really fit by 1 September and I am sure that Mr Lawrence Jones will start you again when it will be up to you to make a great success of your fresh start".

Lawrence Jones was the only executive who was ready to take Bond on his own ground. He probably pushed too hard. On 22 May 1942, he wrote to Bond in Braemar remarking that there had been no letter from him on that day and there must have been a hitch somewhere. He added, "I shall be at my flat every night over the holidays in case you want to get in touch with me or anyone in London".

Bond failed to build a management team and failed to plan his succession. All his life he was in a hurry and single-minded - "hard-driving and impatient" in the words of Marjorie Bond, his niece. Publishing was a personal business in those days. Proprietors were their own chief executives and editors-in-chief. "The truth about Stanley", according to Sir Peter Smithers, "is that he didn't give a damn about anybody. This is what I admired about him. Most people are thrown off course by hostility or criticism or the fear of making fools of themselves. Stanley was not thrown off course by anything or anybody."

All his employees were, in the literal sense, Bond's men. Loyalty to the firm or to him personally had to be absolute. He was a combination of military commander and head of a biblical family; a despot who was also a leader; a father figure who was also an autocrat.

As an innovator, a mover and shaker Bond was pre-eminent. His unwillingness to delegate did not harm the company while he was alive but created a dangerous vacuum after his death. His succession arrangements attempted a balance of power among executives, non-executives and trustees. It was a recipe for discord. It was also a recipe, ultimately, for takeover.

Ron Watson who was the scientific publisher in Butterworths after the Bond era, wrote: "Divide and rule was the technique of Bond's management. He failed in building and organizing a structure which could survive him and continue to expand and flourish after he had gone. He left a perfect takeover situation; a situation unable to withstand the 'corporate' publishing concept which even then had appeared in the USA and within a few years was to cross the Atlantic and change the face of British publishing."

Perhaps so. But Butterworths did remain independent for twenty-five years after Bond's death.

## CHAPTER THREE

## *The Successors*

THE veneer of harmony among Bond's executives did not take long to crack after his death. Like every publishing house, Butterworths in 1943 depended on three pillars - editorial, sales and finance. There is an inbuilt tension among these functions, which requires reserves of diplomacy on the part of the responsible executives if the company is to run smoothly. If this tension is aggravated by personal animosities, the company suffers - unless there is a strong chief executive, the role which Bond had filled. Bond hoped that Kenneth Moore would provide this strong centre. He was right in his estimate of Moore's stature, but underestimated the limitations of Moore's being non-executive, part-time, inexperienced in publishing - and reluctant to take the job.

The three executives who were jockeying with each other in the vacuum of command were E C Leader (brought in by Bond in 1931 as financial officer); the ambitious Lawrence Jones (brought back from Australia on the eclipse of Bellew); and, on the editorial side, the flamboyant John Whitlock who had worked in the company since 1921. There was also a fourth major player on the stage - Seabrook Emery, the company secretary, who was promoted to the Board in accordance with a request in Bond's will. Emery saw himself as a peacekeeper, but while keeping the peace he quietly built his own empire.

Emery's would-be mediatory role is illustrated by a letter he wrote to Kenneth Moore in January 1944, asking Moore to intervene between Whitlock and Lawrence Jones. "Whitlock's attitude," Emery wrote, "is that Lawrence Jones wants all power in his own hands and he has various pieces of evidence to support this view. He mistrusts Lawrence Jones and says that the excuse of the new man coming in and the absolute necessity, therefore, to have the African publishing in the same pigeonhole as the Australian etc, is moonshine." Emery goes on to say that "the crux of the matter is that Lawrence Jones has not enough to do on sales alone, and he knows that he can have no real claim for higher remuneration if he does not do more work. By the same token, Whitlock feels that if he hands over work to Lawrence Jones this cannot improve his chances of more remuneration."

Emery leaned in favour of Whitlock, who, he said, was not really after more money. "Far more important to him is the question of prestige." Emery did not recommend that Jones be given more responsibility. He diplomatically attributed the fracas between Jones and Whitlock to "the effect of four years of war". But it was amazing to him, Emery wrote, "that so much fuss, so much bad blood can arise out of so little."

Emery concluded his letter with the opinion that only Moore "could make it clear to them that they must bury the hatchet for good and all, to drive Butterworths along just as you want it driven." Moore was also hearing frequently from Lawrence Jones, including, for example, an earnest plea, three months after Bond's death, that his allowance of five guineas a week for his London flat should be restored, in view of the fact that his house had been bombed. This was the kind of request that Bond would have settled immediately, probably with a peremptory turndown, but Moore did not have the time or the will to get into such details.

Moore was quite capable of knocking heads together, but he was not close enough to the action. He had no office in the Butterworth premises. The Board meetings were his only exposure. These were genteel and formal, and did not reveal the infighting to the non-executive members (Niekirk, Smithers and Moore himself). The four executive members (Lawrence Jones, Whitlock, Leader and Emery) each had a substantial career stake in Butterworths and all had had working relationships with Bond which each felt gave him an edge over the others.

Into this vacuum of authority was brought, on Moore's recommendation, a man who, without being awarded explicit executive authority, was to dominate the company for six years. Hugh Quennell was a city solicitor, appointed to represent the interests of Hambros Bank, who had purchased, for £231,000, Butterworth shares which had had to be sold to pay death duties on the Bond estate. Quennell became non-executive Deputy Chairman in June 1943. Like Moore, he did not have an office on the company's premises. Unlike Moore, he saw Butterworths as a career and an opportunity, and appointed himself de facto managing director. The interference of this representative of what Whitlock called "the new money" did nothing to improve working relationships. In Quennell's first two years of office he was officially in military service, but, being stationed in London, found the time for Butterworths' affairs. His interventions were too much for Leader, who resigned ten months after Bond's death. He was not replaced. This left Emery in charge of finance. In a sense Emery, Jones and Whitlock were driven closer together by their antagonism to Quennell, whose high-profile management style and flamboyant lifestyle were foreign to the company's conservative traditions.

For example, in 1946 Bond's favourite journal the *Justice of the Peace* attacked the *Daily Mirror* for sending a photographer under a false name to intrude into the privacy of a society wedding. The *Mirror* brought a libel suit against Butterworths which Quennell insisted Butterworths should fight. This was done very expensively, Butterworths hiring two of the most distinguished members of the bar. The case was won, vindicating Quennell's judgment, but thrusting Butterworths into unaccustomed and unwelcome limelight.

Quennell liked the limelight. He had directorships in twenty-three companies, many of them directly connected with the film industry. In his role as chairman of the British and Dominion Film Corporation, he was castigated for insisting on a generous dividend, although the company was making losses. Emery told Barry Rose, editor of the *Justice of the Peace*, about going to the races with Quennell, who was a devotee of the jockey Gordon

Richards. Quennell, Emery related with disgust and alarm, put five hundred pounds on every race.

Quennell's enthusiasm for Butterworths, a pedestrian institution in comparison with film-making, confirmed that Stanley Bond had created a company which was immediately attractive to a financial mind. It was not only secure in its product and its market, but it had a positive cash flow, which could provide either a springboard for expansion, or an attractive balance sheet. Bond, had he lived, would have expanded the company, because he was constantly having new ideas. Quennell also had a lot of ideas, but no experience in publishing, and had to rely on outside advice. His biggest idea was to move Butterworths into scientific publishing, which he attempted under the auspices of a high-powered government committee consisting of distinguished academics. After the end of the war, the British government was anxious to encourage British scientific publishing, partly in the hope of taking over world leadership in this field from the defeated Germans, and partly to reflect the achievements and talents of British scientists, which had been extensively channelled through the United States during the war.

The leading German scientific publisher before the war had been Springer Verlag. With the aid of an editor from that company, Dr Paul Rosbaud, a new company, Butterworth Scientific, was conceived. It was planned that it should enter into partnership with Springer, and become to the world of science what Butterworths already was to the world of law.

The Springer connection drew Butterworths to the attention of a mind more shrewd and substantially less scrupulous than that of Hugh Quennell. Robert Maxwell and Quennell had both served with the Allied Control Commission in Berlin after the war. Maxwell's responsibilities had included the rationing of paper and this brought him into contact with the prostrate Springer. He too formed the idea of re-incarnating Springer in the UK, but as a distributor rather than a publisher. The ambitions of the British government to promote the cause of British science;

Quennell's ambition to make Butterworths a force in scientific publishing; and Maxwell's ambition to build his empire formed an uneasy alliance from 1946 to 1949. Maxwell and Butterworths separately formed joint companies with Springer, Butterworths to publish and Maxwell to distribute. Springer, intent on its own resurrection, wanted shot of both of them.

If Quennell's plans had come to pass, Butterworths might have become not - as Stanley Bond, according to Sir Alex Cairncross, had dreamed - another McGraw-Hill, but at least another Springer or Elsevier. As it was, the Butterworth executives regarded scientific publishing as Quennell's adventure and stayed aloof.

In the Quennell years, Butterworths was also trying to fulfil Stanley Bond's mission to make the company a leading medical publisher. Six months after the war, Lawrence Jones spent a long time in the United States, seeking a US medical publisher to distribute the *British Encyclopedia of Medical Practice*. Long cables were exchanged and reports rendered, but Jones was unsuccessful in his mission, and his recommendations for a limited experiment in the United States at Butterworths' expense were turned down by Whitlock and Emery.

The three of them could have made an effective team under the right command. Emery was a conservative with an instinct for power; Whitlock had charm and ability; Jones had drive. But without teamwork, none of their qualities could be fully realised. In 1948, five years after Bond's death, Lawrence Jones accidentally drove his car into a tree and was killed. Like Leader, he was not replaced. The patient, careful Emery and the impatient, high-living Whitlock had now seen Bellew, Leader and Jones leave the stage. They shared a talent for survival.

One can imagine that there was a tacit agreement between Emery and Whitlock to stay out of each other's hair in their common interest. Whitlock got on with the publishing, while Emery watched the money. Emery's financial role was the source of his power. On 14 May 1947, for example, he submitted a proposal "that some salaries of £600 and upwards were not high enough". He recommended that "Barney" Barns, an accountant destined to run Butterworths' South African company, should be paid £950 instead of £900 in view of the fact that he had "two boys about to be at the expensive stage". Harry Henry, another returnee from Australia, who had been Sales Manager under Lawrence Jones, and whose career in Butterworths was to be peppered with frustrations, might reasonably have hoped that he would be designated successor to Jones, but he was not even recommended for a raise, on the grounds that he had in Emery's words "chosen this of all moments to clothe himself with the mantle of Boobus Britannicus."

In a memo to Whitlock Emery wrote "I know [Henry] finds it hard to make ends meet, yet at £1500 on his present form I cannot help feeling he is adequately paid".

Emery had the habit of writing waspish memos about his colleagues. When Lawrence Jones was visiting Australia in 1947 and sent Emery an account of his visit, Emery passed it to Quennell with a handwritten comment: "This letter is passing strange! I think you should see it because I am anxious for you to realise the atmosphere in which our two colleagues met. Why in the name of all that's sensible does ELJ [Lawrence Jones] want an office outside and if he does why were we not consulted? Nichols [the Australian Managing Director] should be met as a colleague - not as an office boy". Quennell in his reply called it "very disturbing", and said they would "have to watch things carefully".

Emery also kept an eye on Quennell's expenses, which tended to be lavish. Quennell replied from his sick bed to a letter on this subject on 8 March 1948: "I am deeply appreciative of your letter. My secretary, I am bound to say, takes a somewhat gloomy view both of my health and of myself, but I must be allowed to live my own life - as I so often tell her ... This brings me to your memorandum of 3 March on the subject of my remuneration. As you know, I want to suffer equally with you all. All the same, by the simple process of lying in bed and backing Cottage Rake at ten to one I get far more net than I could ever achieve by working in a single day".

Quennell's memos were not always so jovial. One of his instructions to Emery included a coda that "this is a golden opportunity to find our what Douglas Niekirk [one of the trustees] does for his £500". In a "personal" memo of 20 April 1948 to Emery, Jones and Whitlock he stated: "I wish to make it quite plain - if it really requires any further emphasis - that I do not want, and therefore will not have, the head of any one department discussing business and policy with subordinates of another department. All enquiries from one department to another will be made by the head of the one department to the head of the other. If one is away the enquiry will be made through me. This rule is inflexible. Please acknowledge receipt". Emery replied frostily: "I have your memorandum marked personal dated 20 April and as requested I am acknowledging its receipt. I quite understand the contents and will see that they are observed."

Barney Barns, as assistant on Emery's staff from 1946 to 1949 (after which he emigrated to take charge of the South African company), saw at first hand the struggle for power among Quennell, Emery and Whitlock. After he went to South Africa, he received a cable from Quennell giving him unfettered control for two years to carry out proposals he had made about the direction of the South African company. This was quickly followed by a cable from Emery, rescinding Quennell's authority.

Quennell did introduce some modern management into Butterworths, including the much-needed pension plan that Bond would not countenance and a Christmas bonus (4% of payroll). This did not increase his popularity among the managers or the trustees. By 1949, there was a feeling that Quennell had to go and that the only question was the manner of his going. Moore, who had recommended Quennell's appointment, had come to regret it. In a letter to Peter Smithers he complained that Quennell had not only been seen "dead drunk" on the Queen Mary, but that he had "got drunk on liqueurs", which Moore regarded as a particularly disgusting way to do it. "Very able, but quite unstable" is Smithers's summing up of Quennell.

Maurits Dekker, a Dutch scientific publisher who emigrated to the US to co-found the company Interscience, wrote to Kay Jones on 9 February 1978 that Quennell "personified in almost every way John Bull. He scared the hell out of Bob Maxwell. The only one whoever did. Quennell's downfall was tragic; that chapter is wilder than any picture in the wildest novel. The real reasons cannot and should not ever be revealed."

According to Barry Rose, Quennell's dismissal was precipitated by his authorising a loan of Butterworth money on very favourable terms to an advertising agency in which he had an interest. Quennell asked Helen Osborn (who was responsible for the Board minutes, was very much the caretaker of Bond's memory and was the company matriarch) to enter the authorisation of the loan into the minutes, although the Board had not discussed it. Miss Osborn reported this to Emery, who informed Kenneth Moore, and Quennell was fired.

"On Christmas Eve 1949", Kay Jones relates, "Quennell saw senior executives one by one, some in their own offices, some in the Boardroom". He "seemed tired and less aggressive than usual. To Harry Henry he gave a Christmas present better than any box of cigars. He said he intended to return Scientific Sales to Henry's command as from the beginning of 1950. That was Quennell's last appearance in Butterworths' offices."

An Evening Standard clipping headed "Slow Boat to China" reported that "Mr Hugh Quennell, Vice Chairman of Butterworths, has left Butterworths and has decided to take a cruise to China". In fact Quennell was on the way to Australia, and wrote to Moore from there on 14 February 1950 saying that he wished to resign on grounds of health and "to reduce my existing business commitments". Emery had prepared for Quennell's arrival in Australia by writing to the Australian office on 17 January 1950 "that Quennell is, as I write this, on his way to Australia by boat. I do not think it is any secret that he has had more than one breakdown in past years, and, just recently, on very urgent advice, he decided to visit Australia but to do the journey as a means of having a longish physical and mental rest". Emery added that while "at the moment he still retains his connection with Butterworths, there has been some friction in London and he will not be returning". Emery had also written to Quennell on 2 January asking how much expense he could reclaim from Quennell's other interests for trips made to New York in 1949. Emery said after Quennell's departure that he held Quennell responsible for introducing Robert Maxwell to Butterworths, and that the association had cost Butterworths £450,000.

Kenneth Moore felt responsible for Quennell's dereliction, and this was a factor in his own resignation in February 1950. He was replaced by an even more remote city figure, the Earl of Rothes, who knew nothing about publishing.

The final interchange between Emery and Quennell was in May 1953. Emery wrote: "I attach a list of your files that make a parcel about two feet square. Would you kindly let me know whether you would like the whole of the parcel delivered to Tokenhouse Yard, or whether all, or any, of the files may be destroyed". Quennell replied in a one-sentence letter: "Many thanks for your letter. Will you please arrange to have all the files burnt".

Jack Edgerley, Chief Legal Editor, gave Kay Jones this verdict on Quennell: "Quennell had flair, brilliance and could be good company: he was capable of considerable generosity and he wished those who worked for, in effect, him to have a full reward according to the standards of the day. He was prepared to fight for them, when he felt disposed to do so. There was the other side, too: he was a gambler by nature; he was prone to drink; business was money-making only to him; he wished to occupy a "super" position at all times - to take the highest place. I should hesitate to say that he was really trustworthy always, and his nature was one of extremes, including occasionally temper. But he could bring inspiration to people - the spark that helps one to continue with dull labour."

Emery and Whitlock lost no time in reversing Quennell's adventure into scientific publishing. The Butterworth/Springer Company was dissolved and its publications sold to Robert Maxwell for £13,000. Maxwell also hired Paul Rosbaud, the ex-Springer editor, who helped him to found Pergamon Press, on which Maxwell built his fortune. The aborted partnership with Butterworths had given Maxwell insights into law publishing which led to his attempt to buy Butterworths sixteen years later. Pergamon had by that time become a major scientific publisher, its success being built principally on scientific journals, which provide a cash flow comparable with that of law publishing. Maxwell understood money, and how to use it to make more money. Publishing happened to be his vehicle.

Peter Smithers, who by 1950 had become Member of Parliament for Winchester, was also glad to see Quennell go. He had seen his obligations as a trustee from the outset as the preservation of Butterworths so that Ian and Brian Bond (to both of whom he was godfather) would be able to inherit the shares held in trust by their mother and take over management of the company. Since his return from war service, Smithers had found himself willy-nilly keeper of the peace between the Butterworth management and Mrs Bond. This became easier after Quennell's departure, but again more difficult when Kenneth Moore departed. Smithers characterizes Moore's successor, Lord Rothes, as "competent and sound, wholly unimaginative and with no great insight into the workings of the business".

Smithers, from the retrospect of forty years, in retirement in Switzerland, was clear that he "would rather have Butterworths run conservatively and safely than by some powerhouse trying to drive the company forward and double its output at a possible risk".

Of the three trustees whom Bond appointed (Moore, Niekirk and Smithers), Smithers was the one who took his duties most seriously. He was conscientious in keeping in touch with the Bond boys, and in reassuring Mrs Bond that the company was in a healthy state. Myrtle Bond, Smithers recalls, was "very unhappy at board meetings. She understood nothing of what was going on". On the other hand, she never failed to complain to Moore and to Smithers that the company was badly run and that she had no faith in the management. She did not voice these criticisms at the Board meetings, when Whitlock, Emery and Jones were reporting on their stewardship. Understandably, Mrs Bond felt that no-one could match her late husband. As his wife she had lived free of financial cares. Kenneth Moore was deeply hurt by Mrs Bond's criticisms, and both Moore and Smithers looked forward to her replacement on the Board by her new husband, David Willis, whom she married in 1948. Willis was a partner in Willis & Faber, insurance agents. He had met Myrtle Bond as the result of arranging the insurance on her new house, Norton Manor, which Peter Smithers had located for her. But at Board meetings he turned out to be entirely passive, took no part in the proceedings, and made no impression on the other members of the Board.

After the death of Lawrence Jones and the eclipse of Hugh Quennell, no-one stirred the pot. The company became quiescent, stolid and conservative. Mr and Mrs Willis continued to complain and brought pressure on Peter Smithers to agree that some of the trust's shares should be sold. Smithers resisted this strenuously, because he felt it would be a betrayal of the responsibility that Stanley Bond had placed on him. He found placating the Willises very wearisome. Myrtle Bond resented the fact that she did not have sole power over her husband's estate. Her resentment concentrated first on Moore and subsequently on Smithers. It appears that Bond, in his four years of marriage, had not informed his wife of the plans he had made for his estate, or indeed let her know anything about his business. According to

Smithers, "Stanley Bond was not a man who revealed himself unless he had a very, very good reason to do so".

Smithers and Niekirk felt that their duty as trustees was to secure the company's capital. They were not worried that no new ideas were being sprung. The main thing was that no money was being lost, as it had been on the scientific publishing. To the conservative mind, there was a case to be made for confining Butterworths to the cycle of major works and textbooks which Stanley Bond had created. New laws would always be passed; the courts would always be in session; new lawyers would qualify every year. The flow of content would be endless and the market secure. All this had given Butterworths the stability to withstand the losses on the diversification into scientific publishing and to hold together the triangle of conflicting forces - a warring management; dissatisfied owners; and trustees intent on safeguarding their trust.

Myrtle Willis did not see Butterworths' future as part of her duty. She wanted her sons to be financially secure, but David Willis soon persuaded her that there were more profitable ways to invest money than in Butterworths. It is possible that Myrtle Willis did not feel bound by Stanley Bond's wishes, but Smithers and Niekirk did. Bond's letter of 7 May 1942, was addressed to them and said categorically that his sons should "not lightly turn aside their father's work. Rather they should look upon it as a duty to look after their mother's interest in the business and subsequently their own".

Ian Bond knew of his father's injunction from an early age and regarded it not merely as his filial duty, but a course for his life. His brother Brian did not care very much one way or the other, but Ian had inherited the restless ambition and determination of the father he had never known. His mother and stepfather found him hard to handle.

Although Myrtle Willis was not ready to embrace Butterworths' future, she was anxious to celebrate its past. On 16 March 1950,

Myrtle with Ian and Brian Bond

she proposed inviting the entire staff of Butterworths to visit her at Norton Manor. In a letter to Emery, she referred to "my history of Butterworths for which I do hope I shall have your support, because I am quite determined it shall be done". She had collected memoirs from members and ex-members of the staff and had looked around for an author. The idea did not appeal to Emery. "Contemporary history is never much good," he wrote. "We have passed through so many storms that it would be difficult to ignore in any proper history, and even now, I do not think we have the proper perspective on either personalities or events. I myself would like to write the history after my retirement, and I shall provide that it be not published until five years after my demise!" As for the invitation to the staff, Emery said that the Board felt that the party would be too expensive. "There would be upwards of 500 people to entertain," he protested, "and the cost would be at least £1000."

By the early '50s, the post-Bond would-be shakers and movers, for better or worse, had gone. Leader had resigned, Lawrence Jones was dead. Quennell had left in disgrace. Maxwell had been bought off. Kenneth Moore, after a turbulent and thankless seven years, had shed the chairmanship he never wanted. Whitlock and Emery as "joint managing directors" were free to preside, restrained from bickering by their common interest, irked by the constant carping of the Willises, but shielded by the trustees; accepted by Smithers and Niekirk who saw them as safe custodians of the Bond heritage; and responsible only to the benign and gentlemanly Lord Rothes, whose board meetings began at 11.30 am and were over by lunch. The company was in their hands.

Seabrook Emery

John Whitlock

## CHAPTER FOUR

## *The Quiescent Fifties*

MYRTLE WILLIS'S hopes of a history of Butterworths under Stanley Bond survive only as a file of adulatory tributes from his employees. However, her idea of staff gatherings at her home, which Seabrook Emery had vetoed on grounds of expense, survived through the formation, in 1951, of the Old Butterworthians' Society. Its members, initially those who had served before 1938, enjoyed dinners each winter in London and summer expeditions to Norton Manor.

To Mrs Willis these were not exclusively social occasions. At one dinner she informed the audience that "your shareholders are looking critically at the accounts and we must have a greater return on our investment. Therefore there will be changes. Some of you may not like these changes, but these changes will be made because it is necessary for this to be done".

If anyone was to blame for the poor profitability, it was certainly not these troops. Why did she not direct her strictures at Emery and Whitlock? Why not to the Board from which both she and her husband had resigned? David Willis said in his handwritten letter of resignation dated 15th April 1952, addressed to Lord Rothes, that he had to resign because of the demands of Willis Faber, the insurance brokers of which he was a partner. He added that Mrs Willis's "interest in the company and her love for it were as deep as ever" and regretted that she would no longer be represented on the Board.

The criticisms and doubts and suspicions on the part of David and Myrtle Willis were an unexplained mystery to Peter Smithers, who bore the brunt of their discontent. Their complaints seemed so sustained and pointed to be attributable only to Mrs Willis's nostalgia for the Bond era, or to any resentment of a trust she did not control, or to any prompting by David Willis.

Emery          Mrs Willis

Whitl(

Old Butterworthians' dinner 1952

A letter written to David Willis in August 1952 by Sir Patrick Ashley-Cooper provides a possible explanation. It survived by chance from what was obviously an extensive correspondence and fell into the hands of Ian Bond. Sir Patrick had been an old friend of Stanley Bond and a suitor of Myrtle Bond between her marriages.

The letter indicates that there had been considerable dialogue between the Willises and the Trustees. It refers to letters to and from Kenneth Moore, Douglas Niekirk and Peter Smithers. David Willis had apparently sent the file to Sir Patrick, asking his advice.

The letter ("My dear David") reveals that Ashley-Cooper had already been involved and had been making investigations which, he says, "produced a mass of procrastination and incompetence in every direction". He refers to Bull & Bull, Butterworths solicitors, and Edward Moore & Sons, the company accountants as "incompetent and worthless firms". The Trustees, he avers, were all either trying to hold their jobs or had something to hide.

The specific issue on which Willis had sought Ashley-Cooper's advice was the formation of a trrust corporation which would take over some of the family shares, and devise a way in which this could be done without infringing the conditions of the Bond Trust.

Ashley-Cooper does have a good word to say for Kenneth Moore, whom he believes is "an able businessman but ... hopelessly overburdened with his many activities".

Apparently Willis had expressed anxiety about the effect of this proposal on Ian Bond when he achieved the age of twenty-five and entered into his patrimony. Ashley-Cooper reassures him. The plan was to result in the creation of a "trust company" and the sale of non-voting shares to third parties. It was the thin end of the wedge leading to the ultimate sale of the company.

The letter to which Ashley-Cooper is responding had apparently reported that the Bond Trustees were totally against altering the status quo. They had been appointed trustees for three reasons: 1) to ensure that the company was prudently run; 2) to disperse dividends from the Bond shareholding to Mrs Willis; and 3) to maintain the integrity of the company until Ian Bond came of age in 1966.

We may assume that David and Myrtle Willis felt that the income was too small. Her discontent was expressed on several occasions to Butterworth employees who gathered at her home. However, there is no record that either she or her husband, who both had resigned from the Butterworth Board, expressed any criticism of the way the company was run while they were Board members.

Ashley-Cooper's advice was unequivocal: "Get a lawyer!" One with "a fresh untrammelled mind ... who will show you how to get rid of this group, trustees, lawyers, accountants and all and how to appoint and remunerate a trust corporation".

In Ashley-Cooper's opinion, the Willises had been patient too long and had underestimated their power. The situation, he advised, "must be cleaned up once and for all with no sympathy for any of the existing people ... they are much more afraid of you than you can ever be of them".

Ashley-Cooper had been in the picture since Bond died, and, long after this letter was written, was to be instrumental in diverting Ian Bond from Oxford University, where he had been enrolled in accordance with his father's wish, to a location where he would neither receive information nor be able to express his views on Butterworths' affairs.

In his wholesale condemnation of the way Butterworths was being managed, Ashley-Cooper curiously does not mention the managing directors, Seabrook Emery and John Whitlock. He attacks only Smithers and Niekirk as trustees and non-executive directors, and Moore, who had recently resigned as non-executive Chairman but remained a trustee.

The attacks are more ad hominem than against the proposition that a company could be efficiently run by two Managing Directors responsible to a board which was entirely non-executive, met briefly once a month and did not probe into the company's affairs.

Ian Bond believes that Ashley-Cooper "had a huge influence over my mother. He had obviously investigated the position in Butterworths in great detail. I know that my mother was concerned that four of the members of the Board (Rothes, Niekirk, Emery and Whitlock) had sons working in the company and that a case could be made for nepotism".

The outcome of Ashley-Cooper's advice was the formation of a company called BVW Investments Ltd , an investment holding company and Corporate trustee which would be appointed as a replacement trustee for Mrs Willis. The directors of the new company were Ashley-Cooper; Brigadier Sir Henry Holdsworth (another old friend of Stanley Bond); and Richard Millett, a tax lawyer who was David Willis's personal solicitor and had Willis & Faber as one of his clients. Presumably he was the "first-class fighting lawyer" with the "fresh untrammelled mind" that Ashley-Copper had specified.

Nothing changed immediately. The Board, now consisting of Lord Rothes, Peter Smithers, Douglas Niekirk and Philip Mason (ex-Indian Civil Service recommended by Kenneth Moore) – none of whom had any experience in publishing– relied on the competence and stewardship of the two managing directors.

BVW's first request was to sell some of the 46% of the company's shares owned by the Bond Trust. This was rejected by Niekirk and Smithers. BVW then came up with a proposal to split the shares into voting and non-voting. This would enable BVW to realise part of the capital tied up in Butterworths Trust, to enable it to diversify the range of investments and at the same time to satisfy Smithers and Niekirk that the Bond Trust continued to control the company. This scheme was accepted by the shareholders at an extraordinary general meeting in 1955, but a further attempt to capitalise reserves four years later was defeated by minority investors, mainly insurance companies, who objected to the arrangement whereby the Bond Trust retained major voting powers while drawing cash out of the company.

BVW meanwhile had invested the proceeds of the sales of non-voting shares in other businesses. Instructions from Ashley-Cooper, Millett recalled, were that BVW should never hold more than 10% of any one company in its portfolio; should never invest in a company of which the chairman was also the chief executive; and should never invest in any company in the Drayton Group. The Drayton Group was controlled by Lord Rothes.

Throughout the 1950s there was a stand-off between the Bond trustees and BVW, which found itself powerless to implement the managerial changes vaguely threatened by Mrs Willis in her speeches to the old Butterworthians' Society. Whitlock and Emery were the beneficiaries of this stand-off and were able to maintain their partnership until Whitlock's retirement in 1961.

Their collaboration was described by Ron Watson, who was in charge of the sales of scientific books during the 1950s, as "a love-hate relationship between departments which fused into an idolatrous worship of Bond. At the top was the 16th Earl of Rothes, a somewhat nebulous figure. The executive function was exercised by Emery on the financial and administrative side and Whitlock on the editorial and production ... Whitlock was by far the stronger of the two. A 'very likeable rogue' with a Walter Mitty mentality and a great sense of theatre: machismo personified. First introduced to me as Major Whitlock, he belonged to no less than eleven masonic lodges and once received me in his office dressed in the full regalia of a Knight Templar, cloaked in velvet, crowned with a plumed bonnet, a drawn sword in his hand. I liked him, and got on well with him ... Emery and Whitlock ... disliked each other intensely. Emery would tell me of the misdeeds of Whitlock and Whitlock would tell me of Emery's machinations."

Whitlock and Emery were able to work together only because they needed each other; and because neither had a clear edge over the other. Their spheres of influence were delineated. Whitlock was in charge of publishing and North America. Emery was in charge of everything else. They paid long visits to their respective domains. Emery and his wife took four months (October to January) in 1957/58 to visit Australia, New Zealand and Canada, the journey including a three-week vacation and six weeks at sea. Whitlock travelled many times across the Atlantic by the *Queen Mary*.

Some of their correspondence survives. In 1960 Whitlock reported to Emery from Canada that a company founded by ex-Butterworth employee Richard DeBoo was turning over $1m a year. "SSB in his wisdom turned down DeBoo's ideas with scant courtesy, ably assisted by Lawrence Jones. That is how we lost something good." That year Whitlock travelled around Canada with Owen Elliott, whom Bond had despatched to found the company in 1912, and commented that Elliott showed no signs of age. Elliott may indeed have been rejuvenated by finally getting permission to become a publisher, an ambition which Bond had never countenanced.

Whitlock's letters are almost all handwritten on hotel or *Queen Mary* stationery. Emery could not read Whitlock's writing and had to have the letters copied by his secretary. Whitlock's main concerns in his travels were to analyse the management of the Canadian company and to sell American rights of Butterworth medical publications to US publishers, sometimes on terms so generous that the profit was negative, a fact that the assiduous but not always tactful Harry Henry (sales manager but not a director) was at pains to point out in a twenty-five page report in 1957.

The Whitlock/Emery correspondence included banter and laboured goodwill, more on Whitlock's side than Emery's. ("Cheerio, Old Dear, and look after yourself". "I really do miss you, you old so-and-so".) They seemed more comfortable to compliment each other in writing than in direct speech. In one letter, Emery reported that Whitlock's wife had described her husband as "a very great man". While modestly disclaiming such a description, Whitlock, in reply, referred to his and Emery's partnership as "most satisfactory, the like of which would not be seen again". He ended that letter: "I miss your ugly face".

Whitlock's letters convey exuberance. Emery's suggest the thin, tired smile of a burdened man. He ended one letter: "I may be able to write a reasonably good business letter, but I certainly cannot touch you when it comes to writing a chatty social one".

Emery started another letter tetchily: "Since writing last Friday I have received your long, handwritten letter headed 'Wednesday' - the 4th June no doubt - and enclosures; today I have received another long letter from you headed 'Tuesday' - the 10th June no doubt! (I do wish you would write letters like a man and not like a woman!)". Warm sentiments were rare in Emery's letters. Whitlock confessed that he was "apt to be quite voluble on paper and lack that succinct style possessed by my greatest friend, who shall be nameless".

The losses on medical publishing were a frequent topic of the Whitlock/Emery correspondence. Although Bond had started Butterworths in medical publishing in 1935, it was not pursued resolutely after his death. The entry into scientific publishing was regarded by Emery and Whitlock as Quennell's folly. But they continued to do some scientific publishing, and both medical and scientific continued to lose money throughout their regime.

In 1963, with his retirement in sight, and Whitlock already gone, Emery wrote a long apologia in which he took credit for facilitating local publishing by the overseas companies and for the decision to go ahead with the third edition of *Halsbury's Laws.* He blamed the British government for having "encouraged Butterworths to go into scientific publishing" but omitted mention of the disastrous relationships with Springer and Maxwell. During the 1950s, competition in scientific and medical publishing - the former including Robert Maxwell's Pergamon Press the start of which Butterworths had facilitated - had increased markedly. Yet Butterworths continued to do business with Maxwell, selling him distribution rights in the US. In August 1956 Emery wrote to Whitlock: "When I reflect on all that he has had from us and all that you have done, and all the money he has made and is making out of the sales of our works, I just boil. You have received nothing personally and the company has received nothing but kicks. I feel that Maxwell and Nasser (who look a bit alike) must be distant or near relations. [It was the time of the Suez crisis]. I feel that if Maxwell should die on a Monday and - let's face it - you die on the next day, to find myself the trustee of Master Maxwell would cause me to die on the following day: a poor show for Butterworths'.

Views of those who knew Whitlock and Emery vary widely. While to Peter Smithers they were solid and careful, they did little to bring on younger managers. Jack Edgerley, who was Chief Legal Editor, believed that "Whitlock was basically a kindly man and level, not a man of extremes. He genuinely wanted, I think, Butterworths' publications to be good in all respects including the quality of content. But I do not remember his producing in my presence in all the years a single original idea or project. In my relations with him I learnt that I could never expect support if difficulty arose, even when it was merely endeavouring to perform an editorial duty that he had himself assigned to me. He did not give one information that one should have been given, if the title of 'Chief Legal Editor' was to be anything but a name. I have heard Emery express in Whitlock's presence dislike of some of his methods. Whitlock was unwilling to take publishing risks, reasonable risks."

The reason for Butterworths' poor profit record in the 1950s is unconsciously revealed in Emery's elliptic 1963 document. The multi-volume legal works, the creation of Stanley Bond, were making handsome profits and creating a cash surplus, which were used to cover the losses on scientific and medical publishing and to acquire printing and binding companies (Acfords and Woodmans) in Chichester. While continuing to profess great confidence in scientific publishing in his 1963 paper, Emery blamed its lack of progress on Ron Watson who "was not the right man". He adds pointedly that Watson "left when Mr Whitlock retired". Maurits Dekker of Interscience, who hired Ron Watson from Butterworths, wrote to Kay Jones in 1978 that Ron was a good scientific editor but that "Whitlock imposed a nice inferiority complex, and was not willing to have patience ever".

Emery was careful always to make it clear that he had nothing directly to do with either the United States or Canada or with scientific publishing. Whitlock "managed publishing, Canada and United States", while "I took sales, accounts, personnel and day-to-day management, plus Australia and New Zealand, South Africa, Acford/Woodmans and the *Justice of the Peace*".

David Perry, who joined Butterworths in 1955, felt that Emery and Whitlock both regarded themselves in different ways as Bond's heirs. Emery and Helen Osborn (who had been Bond's secretary), Perry recalls, "made a pleasant no-nonsense, competent and (not least) honest administrative team". Emery was there to make the machine run, according to Perry. He did not aspire to be a publisher or a creative person. Whitlock, on the other hand, wanted to fill Bond's shoes, but "he wasn't up to it". Perry, who was to remain with Butterworths until 1973, confesses cheerfully that he was part of the company's nepotic practices, since his brother had been a godson of Helen Osborn.

The consensus of those who worked under Emery and Whitlock is that Emery held the balance of power. "He would not allow anyone to make in-roads into his power base", recalls Barry Rose, who found Emery a jealous and difficult boss. After receiving "an appalling letter", he was about to leave Butterworths when Emery made an apology and withdrew the letter. Rose subsequently discovered that "virtually everyone in the firm of any importance had at one time or another received such a letter from Emery".

Rose blames Emery for numerous lost business opportunities. The company failed in 1960 to acquire Livingstone, the Edinburgh medical publisher, which would have brought Butterworths into the mainstream of medical publishing. The negotiations fell down because Butterworths would not give the Livingstone Managing Director a place on the Butterworth Board. Butterworths also paid too much for Acfords the printers, according to Rose, and fumbled the purchase of the *Police Review*, which was sold to their competitors Sweet and Maxwell. Roland Harris, who had owned the *Police Review*, told Rose that "when I saw Butterworths there wasn't a publisher there". He had dealt with Emery and Lord Rothes. (Rose was a Whitlock supporter.)

Peter Smithers feels that Emery and Whitlock "made a good combination". Emery he recalls as quiet, reflective and responsible, while Whitlock had the drive. If there were any differences between them, they never surfaced at Board meetings. "It may be that in a small circle there are always frictions, but to me they appeared to be a sound team. I never heard either of them suggest what I thought a silly thing and my job was to play it safe and this is what I was doing".

Smithers was, however, critical of Lord Rothes, and, in retrospect, of himself because he did not consider ousting Rothes, which would have been, he had then felt, an unwise gamble. "Rothes was safe and sound and unquestionably honest, even if this extended to getting his son into the company". Smithers did not feel that as a trustee he should be rocking the boat. The more the Willises persecuted him, the more protective he became of what he saw as a safe caretaker arrangement until the day when Ian Bond would step onto the stage.

Ian Bond was twelve years old when Emery and Whitlock commenced their duumvirate in 1952. He had been fostered entirely by nannies and governesses until he was seven, living for his first five years at Braemar Castle, the Deeside manor where his father had been host to many elegant house parties before the war. He saw his mother only on occasional visits, first to Ditcham Park near Petersfield in Hampshire, where his father had lived and next door to which he was buried; and then to Norton Manor, the house which the trustees had found for Mrs Bond.

In accordance with his father's wishes, Ian was deposited in a preparatory school at the age of nine. He was delivered there by his godmother Helen Osborn, who had been Stanley Bond's secretary and became, after his death, the discreet and influential keeper of his flame.

By the end of the 1950s, Ian Bond was on the schedule set out by his father. He had graduated from a successful career at Eton and been accepted at Worcester College, Oxford. Peter Smithers had taken the principal responsibility for preparing the young Bond for the year 1965 when he was due to succeed to his patrimony. But in 1960 there was a sudden departure from the plan. While staying with Brigadier Sir Henry Holdsworth (one of the BVW directors) Ian was informed that he was to go to McGill

University in Montreal, of which Sir Patrick Ashley-Cooper (who was Chairman of the Hudson Bay Company) happened to be a governor. He was being sent to Canada, he was told, rather than the United States, because "his father felt more affinity with Canada". Oxford was not mentioned. "I found it very difficult to accept" Ian Bond recalls. But his passage was booked, and that was that. Initially, he was supposed to go to McGill for one year, but they would not accept him on this basis, so he went on to take his degree there, and was out of circulation when the time came for Whitlock and Emery to retire in the early 1960s.

In spite of this unexplained deviation from his father's programme, Ian Bond's entry into Butterworths was still taken for granted by Smithers and Niekirk and ostensibly by the Willises, and certainly by all Butterworth employees. Ian himself was determined to win his way on his merit. His ambition was sharpened by a serious but unhappy boyhood. He had no home life and found his stepfather David Willis "extremely difficult to get on with". Unlike his younger brother Brian, who had a quiet temperament, Ian was found to be strong-willed and was not wanted at home.

When Whitlock was on a trip in 1960, Emery reported to him that Ian had attended a Board luncheon where he "created a very good impression on everyone. I showed him the Board room and your room and he sat next to the Chairman at lunch. They got on famously".

Emery and Whitlock clearly assumed that Ian Bond would some day (when they were gone) be the Managing Director. This may explain why they do not appear to have given any thought to their own succession. Nor did the next layer of management challenge their regime, with the exception of the ill-starred Harry Henry whom Emery had once referred to scornfully as an overpaid "Boobus Britannicus". In one of his scrawls from Canada, Whitlock compared the veteran Elliott to Henry – "a very good second and marvellous at doing something when asked". Stanley Bond himself had had doubts about Henry. He wrote to Lawrence Jones in 1938: "I have not a very high opinion of this man. It is quite clear that you will have to watch Mr Henry very carefully after you leave him".

By the 1950s Henry was designated General Manager. He had hoped to succeed Lawrence Jones and attain board level, and had considerable credentials. He had joined the company in 1931, when he was chosen from two hundred newly qualified chartered accountants who had applied for a vacancy to replace a man whom Stanley Bond had fired because he declined to work on Saturday afternoons. Henry spent nine months in India in 1933, and ten years in Australia from 1935 to 1945. In the 1950s, he was closer to the staff and to the marketplace than either of the two Managing Directors and was also deeply devoted to the company. According to David Perry, who was Henry's assistant, Henry had a fertile imagination and a creative mind but was unable to delegate and created more work for himself than he could handle. He also had the habit of fighting with people, which accounts for the critical opinions held of him - opinions which frustrated his ambitions throughout his long career with the company.

When Charles Hutt, a scientific editor, resigned in 1956, Whitlock wrote to Emery from Boston: "I don't like the idea of Hutt handing over to Henry one little bit, for it will be so difficult for us afterwards. Why can't Hutt hand over to Watson *temporarily* [Watson was not a favourite of Emery] until I am back - that is a logical thing as I so often consult with Watson - or if you like to Richard [Richard was Emery's son]. But please *not* to Henry. I'll send you a cable to this effect if you like. I am *sure* I am right about this". Poor Henry.

Emery replied: "Watson will be taking over; there is no doubt about that, and we can decide in due course when Henry comes into the picture. I know you would prefer him not to be in it, but it seems to me that it is not good business to keep him out altogether. A lot of time has been spent by him in getting to know something about Scientific, and this would be wasted and we should be totally dependent upon Watson if Henry were now excluded. I am not - neither are you - 100% happy about Watson. I am all for giving him a run, but his obvious shortcomings may not be eradicated. A year from now we may have to think again. I do not mean that we should get rid of Watson, but rather put him back to where he really belongs - the back-room boy's desk". Poor Watson. (But he fared better than Henry, becoming managing director of the British subsidiary of John Wiley, a leading US scientific publisher.)

This exchange between Whitlock and Emery exemplifies the defects of having two Managing Directors. It also illustrates incidentally what Emery meant by including "day-to-day management" in his responsibilities. Emery, awarded a lesser rank than Whitlock in Bond's will, had become by the 1950s the more powerful partner. He was more interested in power than prestige. With Whitlock it was the other way round. Bond's plan had been to diffuse power among three executives - Whitlock (publishing), Leader (Finance) and Lawrence Jones (sales). Emery was to be the watchdog. He became the most powerful executive in Butterworths in the 1950s because he stayed close to the two engine-rooms of the company - legal publishing and finance. Stanley Bond's failure to designate a successor and his faith in the wisdom and judgement of Moore and Smithers had led to a vacuum which Quennell tried to fill. After Quennell was eclipsed, Emery was still there. He surely felt that when Whitlock retired in 1961, his time had come.

The decade of careful but passive rule by Whitlock and Emery proved that Bond had created an impregnable company, one that could have been improved by good management, but could not be ruined by mediocre management. The adventures of Quennell and the attempted intrusion of Maxwell would have sent weaker companies to the wall. Butterworths was not only able to recover, but achieve a modest growth rate. The inbuilt impetus of the company concealed the weaknesses of management, provided a comfortable living and invited complacency. The unsung heroes of the business were the legal publishing staff, most of whom were modest in their ambitions and underpaid, but secure in their tenure and indispensable because of their editorial skills. Whitlock and Emery knew this, but there is no record of their having acknowledged it. In the years after Bond's death, Butterworths' senior management would have been well-advised to recognize the indispensability of those who had come up through the ranks. They needed to have more perception of the professional painstaking, perfectionist publishing which was Bond's concept. Some who became involved quickly perceived the financial beauty of Butterworths, but not all perceived the way in which the good profits were achieved. Bond himself had a financial mind and also a good grasp of the sales and editorial functions, to which he imparted innovation and commitment. The challenge after his death was to maintain these qualities in a management which did not own the company.

Whitlock and Emery were able to preside unchallenged for more than a decade because they understood the company and were responsible to an undemanding board. They did not have to be dynamic. After the turbulence of the 1940s, everybody wanted stability. Emery provided this backstage, while Whitlock, behind the footlights, provided an appearance of leadership. They were rewarded in 1954 by agreements "to secure their services until they respectively reached the age when they are entitled to retire on a pension". They had no boss. They could not be fired. Only death or misdeeds could terminate their employment. Together they were able to paper over the poor results of medical and scientific publishing which should either have been the subject of serious, competent investment or been dropped altogether. As it was, it was treated as a tolerable leak in an otherwise sound vessel.

When Whitlock retired in October 1961, Emery became sole Managing Director. Himself within three years of retirement, he might reasonably have expected that these remaining years would be a peaceful coda to his decades of conscientious stewardship and his ten years of tense shared command. If he and Whitlock had made any plans for their own succession, Emery might indeed have enjoyed a peaceful exit, but he had more travail ahead. In 1962 Peter Smithers, the patient guardian of the Bond Trust, was made Parliamentary Under Secretary to the Foreign Office, a post which required him to resign both as director and trustee, a decision which he may have regretted. This gave the Willises and Ashley-Cooper the opportunity they had long awaited. Richard Millett, the architect of BVW Investments, was elected to the Board.

## CHAPTER FIVE

## *The Turbulent Sixties*

RICHARD MILLETT was a tax lawyer who had set up his own man practice in 1952. When he replaced Smithers on the Butterworth Board in September 1962, he immediately began peppering Emery, who was now the sole Managing Director, with probing questions about the publishing programmes, profits on specific titles, managers' job definitions and performances, salaries, organization, etc. Outspoken by nature,, Millett was not satisfied with the answers. By April 1963 he was accusing the management of under-reporting losses on medical and scientific publishing and the Board of failing to give due attention to the company's accounts. He proposed that they call in consultants to analyse the company from top to bottom.

The Board agreed, confident that they would receive a clean bill of health and that Millett would be discredited. The appointed consultants were Deloittes. The terms of their investigation, which took several months, were unwelcome to Emery and all the Butterworth managers, who had been undisturbed by any serious inquisition since Quennell's eclipse in 1950.

Millett launched his Deloitte proposal in a letter to Emery which concluded: "When the Chairman sees Smithers today and complains to him that this terrible fellow, Millett, has been asking a number of awkward questions, trying to turn Butterworths upside down, I hope that Smithers will refrain from saying 'I told you so'".

Emery's response was to write a three-page single-spaced foolscap memorandum "To the Board", setting out his and Whitlock's record, managing to make it clear that the loss-making operations had been the responsibility of the now departed Whitlock. He defended the poor returns on the Chichester printers and binders and on the recently founded US company, maintaining that the latter, devoted to medical and scientific publishing, would in the end counterbalance the cyclical income from the publishing of major legal works. "At recent Board meetings", Emery concludes his memo, with careful understatement and no direct reference to Millett, "I have gained the impression that doubt seems to have crept in - doubt as to where we stand and even greater doubt as to where we are going. This memorandum will make it clear that we are, and always have been, well aware of our position and are alive to its difficulties and dangers. A great deal of planning has been done, calculated risks have been taken and I trust we shall not falter now, but have the courage to continue on the course we have set ourselves".

The initial Deloitte Report, delivered in October 1963, characterized the information supplied to the Board as "sparse and inadequate by normal standards" and pointed out that there was no system of budgetary control. It concluded that too much depended on the post of Managing Director, and recommended that three executives, responsible for finance, sales and publishing, be elected to the Board.

This recommendation drew attention to the obvious lack of succession. Emery's retirement was due in 1964, and no successor had been designated. The leading candidate was Harry Henry, who had been General Manager since 1952. In his long apologia to the Board, Emery endorsed Henry's cause with restraint, citing his "increasingly valuable help over the years", but made no proposal about his succession.

Millett had specifically criticized the work of Lord Leslie, Rothes' son, who was in charge of scientific and medical publishing and had persuaded Emery to dispense with Leslie's services. At the first Board meeting following the Deloitte Report, Lord Rothes presided with his usual courtesy and dignity until the items concerning the Report and scientific and medical publishing arose when, rising to his feet, he announced: "And now, gentlemen, I bid you good day".

Emery took the chair. Harry Henry was elected to the Board, Deloittes having concluded that he had effectively taken over from Whitlock and should be regarded as Managing Director-elect. After a day's delay, Millett was elected Chairman. For the first time since Stanley Bond had died, there was one person clearly in charge of Butterworths. Millett was determined to shake the company to its foundations.

This appointment was made on Friday November 1, 1963. On the following Monday morning the staff arrived to find Millett literally in office. A group of employees was accustomed to meet at 9 am in the library, which was then situated on the executive floor of the Kingsway offices, for an informal brew-up, organized by the librarian. Leaving the library to refill the kettle, the librarian met a stranger in the corridor: "Can I help you?" he enquired courteously. "I'm your new Chairman," came the reply. "Tell me: what time does this floor come alive? And why are you carrying a kettle?" The other members of the tea group diplomatically snatched up piles of papers and passed this unexpected new broom in the corridor with a polite "good morning". Millett's meticulously kept diary recalls that he arrived at 8.50; a typist at 9.05; and the librarian at 9.12. He met Henry in the central hall at 9.17. He found little to please him in his first hour as chairman. But he had much deeper problems than timing staff arrivals.

Deloittes had diagnosed the company, but not offered a cure. On the publishing side, they knew no more than Millett. They could pinpoint the poor returns, but were not able to analyse inadequacies of list-building which had led to the poor returns. Equally, to require that senior executives be elected to the Board was one thing. To identify those executives was another. This was the subject of a prolonged wrangle between Millett and Henry. After the Deloittes Report, one might have expected a bloodbath, but the only persons to leave were Lord Rothes and his son. Millett was left in a state of frustrated confrontation with the management. His principal target was the unfortunate Henry, who wanted to be confirmed as Emery's successor and to have his nominees elected to the Board. Millett wanted to bring in fresh blood. They fought for several months, with Deloittes as mediators. In the end they agreed to create a separate "management board", with Henry as the only member of both boards. Kay Jones describes the result of this device as follows:

> Five senior executives were summoned to meet Emery and Henry on 26 February 1964: they were Phil Hogger (Accounts); Jim Marsden (Sales); David Jollands (Medical and Scientific Editorial); and Jack Edgerley and Kay Jones (Legal Editorial). They were told that, if the shareholders agreed to the amendments, they would be appointed the first Executive Directors. Emery was to be Deputy Chairman, and Harry Henry Managing Director.

> The Executive Directors were given letters in which they were asked to 'play a greater part than heretofore in recommending policy and assisting the Board and the Managing Director to agree upon and formulate policy'. Their views would normally 'be channelled to the main Board through the Managing Director and *vice versa*, but where policy matters in spheres over which they have direct responsibility are to be discussed at meetings of the main Board, they will be invited to attend'. They were reminded that 'the office of Executive Director will not attract any remuneration as such'.

After a few months, Henry elected to return to Australia as Managing Director there. Harry Henry was the "nearly" man of the Butterworth post-war management. He had returned to the UK in 1945 after ten years in Australia to find his ex-boss Lawrence Jones one of the post-Bond anointed. After Jones's death, he became "General Manager" to the Whitlock/Emery duumvirate, but was never admitted to the secretive Boardroom club. Yet to the publishing world, Henry was the best-known face of Butterworths. He knew the business intimately and worked tirelessly. Having assumed Whitlock's responsibilities, he could be excused for expecting that his thirty years of service would entitle him to be Emery's successor.

He had believed at first the he could work with Millett. On the evening after the Board met to consider the Deloittes Report and dispersed without electing a new Chairman, Henry received a telephone call from Mrs Willis enquiring "whether I felt I could work with Millett as Chairman". Henry replied that he would rather have Millett than an unknown outsider. After all, the Managing Director, he thought, not the Chairman of the Board, would be running the company. "What a colossal misjudgment I made!" he wrote twenty years later in a letter to Kay Jones, in whose history he felt he had been done less than justice. Jones, who had joined Butterworths in 1934, three years after Henry, had no intention of maligning his old colleague. When Kay Jones was researching the history in 1978, Millett told him that he had "found ... notes and correspondence which make it quite clear that the low morale at Butterworths, if it was low, and my bad image with the staff, if bad, was largely due to Henry." Millett's distrust of Henry is illustrated by Henry's account of his unheralded arrival in Sydney in 1967. According to Henry:

The Wentworth Hotel is only a few minutes' walk to the Butterworth offices. I don't know for certain, of course, but I imagine that sometime in the afternoon Millett did a 'recce' to locate Butterworths. After that he awaited till it was dusk (about 5.30 pm in Sydney in August) and then he slunk quietly down to Lofters Street. The office was shut, but there was a light on on the first floor, so Millett goes and thunders on the front glass door, but could gain no attention. So he crosses the road to a small triangular park opposite and picks up a supply of pebbles, rocks etc and starts heaving these at the first floor windows. This time he does attract attention. Bruce McKenzie goes down to see what is going on, and Millett introduces himself as the Chairman of Butterworths from London, and asks to see "Henry's room." McKenzie explains that I am not there. (My wife and I had taken Howard Drake of London University - an old friend - out to dinner). Millett replied that he does not wish to see me, but my room. He is taken up to my room where he then proceeds to take two hours going through all the papers and files in my room!

McKenzie rang my house, and my daughter rang the restaurant, and after speaking to her I returned to our table laughing. My wife did not think it a joke, and certainly Howard Drake was shocked when I told them that Millett at that moment was in my office presumably rummaging through my papers, but Millett's code of ethics was a source of never ending amazement to me.

The next day, Millett turned up early at the office, but I was there before him. His excuse for being in Sydney was that he wanted to approach Bill Nichols and offer him a Joint Managing Directorship - ie joint with me! I refused to discuss it with him. I knew Bill would turn the offer down.

I drove Millett to the airport. His plane was held up so we had a short wait, during which he told me he had decided not to make any offer to Bill Nicholls. He also started talking about his Chairman's speech and I told him that if he continued using it as an invitation to small publishers to join Butterworths, it would probably result in a large publisher making a bid for Butterworths. 'Nonsense' he said. 'Nonsense'.

Millett's report to the Board confirms this account in substance, but he observed mildly on reading the Henry letter that he did not "slink quietly" or "thunder" on the door. He added that his visit to Butterworths was incidental to his trip to Australia on behalf of another client.

Henry's banishment to Australia left Millett as de facto Managing Director, a situation from which he was eager to extricate himself. He was a part-time employee and still had his legal practice. He set out to recruit a managing director, but felt he was impeded by the fact that Butterworths was seen as a family company in which the top job would go to a family member.

Certainly Ian Bond, now back from McGill University and approaching his twenty-fifth birthday, believed that Butterworths was his destiny. He suspected that Millett's real intention was to install new management and then sell the company. While maintaining that his mandate was simply to improve the company's performance, Millett did have discussions with outside parties, based on the assumption that Butterworths would be the acquirer or at least an equal partner.

In his public pronouncements on becoming chairman Millett reported on his clean-out of nepotism in Butterworths and on how his knowledge of tax laws had improved Butterworths performance. If he did not put the company explicitly on the market, his high profile, including speeches about warding off American predators and affirming that Britain had too many publishing companies, indicated a readiness to receive approaches.

To Ian Bond, Millett expressed the view that he should prove himself elsewhere before joining the family company. Bond, for his part, had no desire to enter Butterworths with a silver spoon. During his three years in Canada, he had travelled widely in the United States, studied American publishing, and worked in the Butterworth companies in Washington and Toronto. On his

Ian Bond

return from Canada to the UK in 1964, he applied for a job at the British branch of McGraw-Hill. Told there was no vacancy, he presented himself at McGraw-Hill's offices in Maidenhead and asked to see the author of this book, who was the Managing Director. I saw him, was impressed, and took him on as a trainee, on condition he started to work in the warehouse.

Bond did not reveal his connection with Butterworths and I had no knowledge of it. For the next six months, driving daily the thirty miles from London, Bond acquired a lot of calluses and learned a lot about books by handling them. After six months he was promoted to be a college traveller, and was regarded as a promising employee. I was in the habit of hiring ambitious graduates from universities in the knowledge that most of them would move on to other companies after a few years. So when Bond left after two years, I was not surprised.

I would have been surprised had I known that, while working at McGraw-Hill, Bond reported to Richard Millett what he was learning about the publishing business. Millett, thirty years later, denied any such conversations took place. Bond maintains that Millett was conscious of his lack of experience in publishing, and wanted ostensibly to improve his own performance, but actually to groom Butterworths for sale. This fits in with a phone call that I received from Richard Millett asking if I would be interested in becoming Managing Director of Butterworths, and with Millett's reference in a public pronouncement to the rapid sales progress of the British branch of an unnamed American corporation.

In the summer of 1966, Bond was asked by his mother and stepfather to leave McGraw-Hill and join Butterworths. He left McGraw-Hill with that intention. Having attained the qualifying age of twenty-five, he had now taken over as a trustee of his father's estate from his mentor Peter Smithers. Having gained two years of experience in publishing, he felt that he was entitled to a job in Butterworths on his merit. To his surprise and dismay, Millett declined to hire him. He had made a number of public pronouncements against nepotism and claimed that employing a Bond would undermine his stand. Ian Bond could reasonably have expected his mother and stepfather to intervene vigorously on his behalf, but they did not, and a bitter quarrel ensued. He was now barred from his father's company and unable to get a serious job in any other company, because it was presumed that his future lay in the family company.

He protested vigorously to Millett. When he left McGraw-Hill, he had received a letter from the Editor-in-Chief asking him to reconsider his decision. He showed this letter to Millett and said, "if they would have me, why won't you?" During his two years in McGraw-Hill, Ian Bond says, Millett was quite friendly, but he changed his attitude abruptly when Bond left McGraw-Hill. The Willises had not informed Millett that they were instructing their son to leave McGraw-Hill to join Butterworths. They could have insisted on his acceptance, but apparently were afraid of offending Millett and losing his services. Both the Willises had reason to be grateful to Millett for devising BVW Investments.

Millett laid it on the line with the Willises that they could either have Ian Bond or him. When becoming Chairman of Butterworths, he had written to Mrs Willis: "as for my being there for a very long time, as you know, you have the power at any time so to arrange matters that by agreement between you and your son I could be removed overnight". When the crunch came in July 1966, the Willises came down on Millett's side. They knew by this time that the company was likely to be sold, but hoped Ian would be given a chance to make his mark before the ownership changed. Ian was resolutely against the company being sold. It would be "a betrayal of my father's wishes". This caused tremendous acrimony. By Christmas 1966 Bond was expelled from the family home and all communication with his mother and stepfather ceased.

In desperation, Ian Bond consulted scions of other British publishing houses, including Billy Collins and Mark Longman. From the latter he learnt that Millett was having discussions about "a merger" which would in fact be a takeover. He told Longman he could not support this.

David Willis was deeply torn by his stepson's rejection. On 15 November 1966 he wrote to his stepson that he had "spent many hours and sleepless nights endeavouring to find a formula which is fair and reasonable to all concerned to overcome the difficulties that have arisen with Mr Millett regarding your and our wishes that you will be able to enter Butterworths as soon as can reasonably be expected". However, Millett had written to Willis on 8 November that he had not changed his views and that "the only choice appears to lie between my withdrawing my opposition and there being a flaming row which might well split Butterworths down the middle. Either choice would in my opinion be bad for Butterworths and undo much of the good, if any, that I have been able to effect since I joined the Board." Ian Bond could enter Butterworths on January 1, 1968 [more than a year away] but "between now and the end of 1967 my successor will have to be found."

Willis's reply temporised. "To my mind it is essential for an amicable agreement that the family would agree to sell the bulk of their personally owned shares. The company could be sold, but Ian could go to work there anyway." Ian had neither the financial muscle nor the persuasive power with his mother to prevail. The breach was now irreparable.

Looking back on these events, Millett wrote to the author in 1992:

I do not think the Willises had appreciated that the management was as bad as it was – they probably had no yardstick to judge it by. I do not believe that anyone in Butterworths looked at the figures of their competitors, even if they were available. I do not know when Longmans floated, but I remember, at one time, I compared Longman's share price with Butterworths over a period of years, from which it was clear that any investor who had put his money into Longmans would have seen it increase in value more than Butterworths – six times if my recollection is not at fault.

The Board members were very satisfied with themselves. Emery told me, after Rothes left, that the Board had only agreed to management consultants being brought in because the Board was confident that it would be given so good 'a bill of health' that I would feel obliged to resign.

Ian Bond had had a danger signal in November 1963 when Peter Smithers resigned from the Board. He wrote to Ian in Canada that he had "expressed the view to Mr Millett that you should come home immediately in order to discuss fully the appointment of a new Chairman, and I said that I thought you should be separately advised on this vital matter by somebody not obviously personally interested. Mr Millett then informed me that he himself wished to be Chairman of the Company until such time as you could yourself take over, which would be in about ten years' time. He also informed me that it was the wish of your mother and of yourself and Brian that he should do so. He did not think it was necessary for you to return".

Smithers (then still a trustee) and Niekirk, who was still both trustee and Board member, agreed. Smithers wrote further to Bond: "There is no urgency for the appointment of a Chairman. This is a matter which requires very careful thought and investigation; and you yourself should be separately advised about any names put forward. As, however, in my view the decisions about your affairs are now for yourselves to take in the family ... I took no further action and Mr Niekirk did not oppose the election of Mr Millett, although he asked for his views to be put on record". Smithers concluded: "It may well be that all will turn out for the best, but I must tell you that I do not think such very important matters ought to be decided in this way". He perceived the danger, but felt powerless to do anything about it. He had been guardian of Stanley Bond's wishes and Ian Bond's expectations for twenty years as godfather, trustee and Board member, but had been outmaneuvered by the insertion of Millett.

Millett was acting, of course, on behalf of Myrtle Willis, who may well have felt that her husband's will treated her more as the mother of his children than as his wife. Apparently Stanley did not share with her the contents of his will, drawn up six months before his death. Myrtle Willis no doubt wondered why Ian could not be like Brian, her younger son, who had no interest in joining Butterworths and took a job in his stepfather's company. Ian saw Butterworths as his destiny and its sale as a betrayal of his father's wishes.

Millett wrote in 1992: "Mrs Willis did not appreciate 'that Butterworths, in the 1960s, was a very different animal from the time when Bond ran it. As a result of the share re-organization, on a capital basis the public's interest was double that of the Bond Estate'".

He added: "After Ian left McGill University – why McGill, not Oxford, I do not know - I never saw any CV – he asked to be engaged by Butterworths. I gave him the advice which I knew other clients had given to their sons, viz make your mark elsewhere for, say 5 or 10 years, and then come in at an appropriately higher level when, by your experience, you would gain the respect of the other employees. It was I who recommended that he should go to McGraw-Hill and the first I knew of his leaving McGraw-Hill was when David Willis told me, and said that his wife wished me to employ Ian in Butterworths. In my view, the introduction into Butterworths of Ian Bond at that time would have been disastrous to morale and would have put an end to my hope of finding and introducing a new Chief Executive."

The public's interest consisted of non-voting shareholders and Hambro's bank, which had expressed no discontent with the modest profit performance in the Emery/Whitlock years. Millett was not ready to agree that the intention to sell Butterworths dated from the strictures of Ashley-Cooper and the formation of BVW Investments and was blocked only by Peter Smithers until he was replaced on the Board by Millett.

Ian Bond believes that by 1966 events had moved too fast for Millett and "he felt trapped as far as I was concerned and furthermore that the morale within Butterworths was extremely low and there were still many employees in the company who would liked to have seen me working there in some capacity. Millett may have thought that this could have been divisive".

Rebuffed by Millett and ostracized by his family, Ian Bond decided to go to Australia and work for his old friend Harry Henry. He thought that this might demonstrate to Richard Millett that he didn't wish to become Chairman. "I didn't even wish to become a Director. I wished to work my way up in Butterworths as I had in McGraw-Hill".

In the course of his (unpaid) work in Australia, Bond was assigned by Frank Judson, a veteran editor who had worked for Stanley Bond in England and in India, to travel round Australia and gather material for a booklet on the Australian mining industry. At an Old Etonians' dinner in Sydney, he met the Chairman of Western Mining, one of the companies which he had visited. On his advice, he invested the legacy he had received on his twenty-fifth birthday in Western Mining and later in Poseidon, companies which were about to boom due to the demand for nickel at the time of the Vietnam war. As a result, he quickly became, in his own words, "a rich young man", and decided to return to England with the intention of either acquiring a substantial equity in Butterworths, or failing that, of starting his own publishing house.

Ian Bond's presence in Australia did not please Richard Millett. Bond theorizes that Millett's unannounced arrival in Sydney and his rummaging through Harry Henry's desk was in the hope of uncovering some plot that he imagined Henry and Ian Bond were making.

On 29 March 1967 Bond wrote to Millett:

Please put clearly and plainly in writing your cogent reasons for forbidding me to work with Butterworths, both in

London and in Australia. Neither my family nor myself have ever understood your unbelievable attitude in this respect for several reasons:-

1.    You have frequently emphasized the principle of acceptance on merit.

2.    None of my family are in Butterworths in any capacity. Thus, my entry would in no way contradict your public statements about nepotism, your attitudes to which have grown right out of proportion, and have abused all principles of democracy and fairness.

3.    Before you succeeded Lord Rothes as Chairman, it was made very plain to you that I intended to make my life in Butterworths after some experience outside, which you readily accepted. This you can never deny.

4.    You have confided in me all matters of policy of Butterworths, asked me my advice on vital decisions.

I ask you now, for the last time, NOT to brow-beat my poor mother or stepfather. They are not only fed up but it is a pointless exercise on your part, as I shall never agree to any change as far as Butterworths is concerned, particularly since you seem to be using this to forbid my entry into Butterworths. This was the greatest stab in the back my family have ever experienced, for a career in Butterworths was not only the will of my father and the life-long ambition of my mother, but was accepted, as I understood, by you.

Millett replied on 14 April 1967:

I have your letter of 29th March. As you request me to speak plainly, I will do so.

I would not employ you in Butterworths in either England or Australia if your name were not Bond. The reasons are simple and, I am very sorry to have to say, are firstly that I am afraid I no longer have any confidence in you and, secondly, I do not think that it would be in the interests of the Company to employ you at the present time. Since this is how I feel, then, whether my views are justified or not, it would be wrong of me to depart from them simply because you are a trustee or a shareholder.

To answer fully the remaining remarks in your letter would take more time than I am able to devote just now. Briefly, however, my comments on the remaining remarks are as follows:-

1. Acceptance on merit: agreed.

2. Abuse of principles: This is a matter of opinion and I disagree with yours.

3. I disagree entirely. On the contrary, you made it quite clear at that time that you would not wish to become a whole-time Managing Director of Butterworths - having regard to the likelihood that you would enjoy a very substantial private income - but that you would like to fit yourself to succeed me as Chairman of that company. Accordingly, while you were at McGill I urged that you should study accountancy and I think I mentioned that a Chairman of a company such as Butterworths must be able to understand accounts, otherwise he would be in danger of repeating the foolishness of Smithers who joined in congratulations to all concerned in the Scientific Department for the results achieved when those results were an improvement in the gross profit ratio from 17.7% to 17.8%, both of which percentages fell far short of the amount required to show a profit. Subsequently, after joining McGraw-Hill you may well have changed your mind, but it was always understood that you had accepted the principle which I advocated, namely that you should make your name elsewhere and then come into Butterworths at a high level if you were then fitted to do so. The idea that you should come in at the bottom and work your way up was anathema to you as recently as 1965.

4. As a Trustee of the Bond Estate I have discussed certain matters with you, but to suggest that I asked your advice on

any vital decision is not correct. You had no experience at all otherwise than as a College Rep. What important advice could you possibly give me?

"Brow-beating your family": this allegation is untrue.

"I shall never agree to any change so far as Butterworths is concerned". I have tried to help you to see matters in the light of the 1960s, not the 1930s. I have clearly failed. Butterworths is a public company and the family have sold a large number of shares to the public, to whom they owe a duty and to whom I, as Chairman - and indeed all the other Directors - owe a duty. It is not our duty that the company should be kept inviolate as a family preserve until such time as you can persuade your family to exercise such votes as they may then have to enable you to head it. I have noted what you say but unless and until I receive a unanimous directive from the Trustees to the contrary, I shall recommend to the shareholders and the Board of Butterworths to take such steps as I consider to be in the interests of the shareholders as a whole. If I receive a unanimous request from the Trustees to do anything which I consider contrary to the interests of the shareholders as a whole, then I shall naturally have no alternative but to place the facts before the shareholders so that they may judge.

By 1967, as a result of the approach by Robert Maxwell, Millett was both entertaining and seeking alternative offers. He perceived this as "in the best interest of the shareholders". In the perspective of what was going to happen to British publishing in the next ten years, he was right. The era of family publishing firms was coming to an end, and with it the employment of the children of the founders. Collins was sold to Rupert Murdoch's News International, a move which members of the Collins family brought about. Longman, which was considering acquiring Butterworths (and which did acquire Penguin) became a division of Pearson. After Mark Longman died, there was no Longman in Longman.

Ian Bond accepts that the end of family ownership was inevitable, but believes that he was unfairly blocked from the opportunity to prove himself on his merits. Richard Millett did not dispute that he had blocked Ian Bond and "in the circumstances would have done it again". He claimed to know nothing of Stanley Bond's wishes for his sons, but "assumed that it would have been his wish that one or both of his sons should go into the business, whether they were suitable or not".

During his five years as Chairman of Butterworths, Millett was unpopular with everyone in Butterworths. He saw it as his job to shake up a complacent, sleepy company, and didn't care whom he offended in the process. The history of Butterworths from the time of the founder's death until the accession of Millett illustrates that there is no substitute for strong leadership. A company is a hierarchy, not a commune, and there is no more corrosive recipe than a compliant non-executive board and a management which sees the company more as a living than a career.

Butterworths' profit record showed significant growth under Millett's command, pre-tax profits rising from £390,000 in 1963 to £506,000 in 1966, figures achieved after stock write-offs of £503,000 in 1963-65. The prudent Millett wrote off much more in three years than had been written off in the previous seven.

What Seabrook Emery, by this time a powerless witness of the Millett reign, thought of these figures, is not recorded. He and Whitlock had failed to gain the confidence of the owners and by failing to groom successors, had made Millett inevitable.

## CHAPTER SIX

## *The Takeover*

ROBERT MAXWELL'S first contact with Butterworths was through John Whitlock in the immediate post-war years. Both enjoyed maintaining their wartime ranks in peacetime. In 1949 Major Whitlock introduced Captain Maxwell to Sir Charles Hambro, whose bank was a substantial shareholder in Butterworths as a result of the purchase of part of the Bond estate to pay inheritance taxes following Stanley Bond's death in 1943. Butterworths had recently launched itself as a scientific publisher. Maxwell had offered his services to Springer Verlag, the German scientific publisher, to build its export markets. He needed capital. Sir Charles lent him £25,000.

Shortly thereafter, Butterworths approached Springer, prompted by Dr Paul Rosbaud, a pre-war Springer employee, who had been instrumental in helping Butterworths start in scientific publishing. Behind this move was Hugh Quennell, Deputy Chairman and representative of Hambro's interests on the Butterworth board, who had known Maxwell when they were both in the Allied Control Commission in Berlin. A triangular relationship between Butterworths, Springer and Maxwell then ensued.

When Quennell was eclipsed, Butterworths were anxious to get out of its partnership with Springer, and sold its scientific publishing list to Maxwell for £13,000. Rosbaud went with the deal and was valuable to Maxwell in building, in its early days, the business which became Pergamon Press.

Robert Maxwell continued during the 1950s to have commercial dealings with Whitlock, who served as a Maxwell trustee for a time, and with Emery, although he was deeply suspicious of Maxwell and bitter about the amount of money he claimed Butterworths had lost through the Maxwell association.

After Millett became Chairman in 1963, Maxwell, whose Pergamon Press by this time was the largest publisher of scientific books and journals in Britain, frequently called him seeking an interview. There was a meeting in 1966 about a merger of Butterworths and Pergamon, an idea which Millett, according to Maxwell, did not dismiss. There was also talk of Pergamon distributing Butterworths' scientific and medical books in the United States. Maxwell felt rebuffed or ignored and wrote about his discontent to Millett on 26 September 1967.

Apparently they had met over lunch at the Savoy when, according to Maxwell, Millett expressed his "concern at the mounting losses of Butterworth, USA and asked whether I would be interested in taking it over". Maxwell says that he immediately agreed to do this but heard nothing further until "you closed it down and turned over the distribution to Messrs Consultants Bureau". Pergamon, Maxwell claimed, could "sell more Butterworth scientific and medical books than Consultants" and moreover, the profits from a Pergamon agency, Pergamon being a UK company, "would have helped the national balance of payments".

Maxwell went on to claim that Millett had offered Butterworths' US agency to McGraw-Hill, who had turned it down, and in the final paragraph of his letter fired his big gun: "You will remember that I offered to merge Pergamon with Butterworths some two years ago, under your chairmanship. You said that it could be interesting but that you preferred to see first what you could do with Butterworths on your own. You are entitled to reject an offer to merge with Pergamon, but why must that decision prevent you from offering your American distribution and/or scientific and medical list to Pergamon in the interest of Butterworth shareholders?"

Since he was "desirous of a prompt response" Maxwell "took the liberty" of copying his letter to Seabrook Emery "whom I have known and dealt with on Butterworth/Pergamon affairs for many years". Maxwell, not the most sensitive of animals,

74

was apparently unaware that as a result of these dealings, Emery disliked him intensely.

If Maxwell was looking for a fight, he had picked the right man. Millett's reply was long, detailed, feisty, and at the same time cautiously included legal safeguards. It is worth quoting in full, because it reveals a lot about Millett, and also poses the question of what Millett was trying to accomplish. Did he just want to provoke Maxwell, and establish his own rectitude, or did he aim to precipitate a hostile bid?

I have your letter of 26 September. My comments are as follows:

1.    In June 1964 you invited me to be Chairman of a merged Butterworth/Pergamon undertaking and I declined because I did not consider it to be in the interests of Butterworths to merge with Pergamon.

2.    The only lunch that took place was in July 1964 shortly after Pergamon went public, and when you will remember the Prospectus disclosed that your staff was 420, whereas a few months earlier your catalogue had shown it was 750. I well remember remarking that I thought that our management consultants who had recently come into Butterworths at my request were doing a good job but they had not been able to recommend any reduction of the magnitude which you had apparently achieved - you must have had advance notice of SET [Selective Employment Tax] or was it that the 750 was a mild exaggeration?

3.    In November 1964 you repeated your proposal with the same result. I heard nothing further from you until February 1966 when you again telephoned me and enquired as to the prospects "of the family merging Butterworths with Pergamon" and urged me, in effect, to persuade the family trustees to do a deal with Pergamon behind the backs of the other shareholders leaving them to come in afterwards if they wished to do so. You will remember you pointed out that while the new Companies Bill then recently introduced

into Parliament did not abolish non-voting shares, a new Bill would be introduced within 12 months which would forbid non-voting shares and that therefore the Trustees' holdings would diminish in value and therefore now was the time to sell. During the same conversation, the 1965 Finance Act was discussed in relation to copyright and close companies, and my success in achieving an important amendment to the Finance Bill - see Hansard 12 July 1965, col 104.

4.    Since that date my office cannot trace any record of any telephone call or attempted telephone call from you to me until, as mentioned below, May 1967 when, following the appearance of this paragraph in the Daily Mail, viz

'Mr Robert Maxwell of Pergamon Press is to reopen bid talks with Butterworths, the legal, medical and scientific publishers'

I received a message from you through your brokers Rowe & Pitman on 22 May to the effect that if I wished, you would come to see me and no doubt you received the message back to the effect that as I had already told the Daily Mail there was no truth in the reference, there was no object in our meeting. I do not know whether you or your secretary received that message, but on 25 May you and/or your secretary telephoned my office when I was out, and my secretary asked that if you had anything to say to me would you put it in writing. Since you did not write, I concluded that - for once - you had nothing to say.

5.    I do not deny your having expressed an interest in buying Butterworth Inc if it was ever for sale, but you have no right to reproach me for not having offered it to you or accuse me of having "turned over the distribution to Messrs Consultants Bureau". The short answer is that Butterworth Inc has not been sold, is not for sale, and that we have made no arrangements for the distribution of Butterworth's books in the States by Messrs Consultants Bureau. Indeed we would not have been so stupid as to place all our US

distribution in the hands of one company. On the contrary, after a long and careful survey we made arrangements with a number of firms selected by us as being in our opinion best suited to distribute Butterworth books within a certain field on terms considered to be satisfactory to us, eg Lippincott for Clinical Surgery, a major work which I should hate to see your Encyclopedia salesmen attempting to handle; Appleton Century for certain non-medical major works; Plenum for certain scientific titles, and so on.

You claim that Pergamon can do a better job than Consultants Bureau in distributing our books in the States. As Consultants Bureau have not been appointed our distributors, your claim, even if true, is irrelevant. Whether Pergamon would have done a better job than those companies whom we have appointed our distributors is a matter of opinion. If, however, Butterworths had thought it was in the interests of the shareholders of Butterworths to appoint Pergamon its US distributors, I would have approached you to negotiate terms. I did not do so and I do not know any other UK publisher for whom Pergamon acts as distributors in the States.

6.    With reference to your enquiry, the Board of Butterworths sees no attraction to Butterworths, its staff or shareholders in a merger with your company.

Having said this, I must also say that I prefer a direct approach to learning of your intentions, real or alleged, either  from the press, or through a fellow-Director or in some other unorthodox manner.

If and when, however, Pergamon decide to make a takeover bid for Butterworths, whether or not that bid is to be accepted will be decided not by the Butterworth Board but by the shareholders. In order, however, to avoid abortive expenditure and a mass of circulars, I think it only right to tell you that in my opinion:

(a)   If the offer envisaged any exchange of Butterworth shares for shares or other securities of Pergamon, it is highly improbable that the holders of the majority of the voting shares would even consider it.

(b)   If the offer were for cash and the holders of the majority of the voting shares were tempted to accept such a bid from Pergamon, which in my opinion is also highly improbable, I don't consider that the bid would achieve your purpose because I am confident that Pergamon would be outbid.

7.   I think I have dealt with all the relevant points which you have raised, but being a prudent lawyer and in case I have omitted to deal with any point, I should state that - save as set out in this letter - I make no admissions on any of the contents of your letter.

8.   Although you marked your letter, or rather the envelope "Private and Confidential", you sent a copy to Mr Emery and, in the final paragraph, stated that this was an official communication to the Butterworth Board. I accordingly placed your letter before the Board and, to save you the trouble of showing this reply to your Co-Directors, I am sending to each of them direct a copy of this letter.

Maxwell's reply, dated 6 October, consisted of a single sentence:

On behalf of myself and my colleagues I return your communication of September 29 as being impertinent, untrue and totally unacceptable.

In the light of this exchange, the fourteen-page prospectus entitled "Offer by Henry Ansbacher & Co Ltd on behalf of Pergamon Press Ltd for the 'A' Ordinary, 'B' Ordinary and Preference Shares of Butterworth & Co (Publishers) Ltd", dated 23 October 1967, must have come as no surprise to Millett and the Butterworth Board.

Millett had now been Chairman for four years. Harry Henry had gone to Australia two years earlier, in October 1965. There was no Managing Director. Ian Dickson had been recruited from Penguin as Financial Director and elected to the Board in June 1965. Kay Jones had replaced Whitlock who had continued on the Board as non-executive until 1966. Millett had spoken many times about the need to bring in new and younger executives. Several had joined, but only Ian Dickson at Board level. Millett was effectively Managing Director, although he was a part-time employee and still in practice as a tax lawyer.

Millett had been talking to Longman about a merger. He told Kay Jones in 1977 that "Mark Longman was very keen on the idea, but had to withdraw when Maxwell came on the scene because he was vulnerable". Millett believed that Longman was so frightened of Maxwell that he "rushed into the arms of the Financial Times", which Millett saw as "a damn shame, because Longman would have made an excellent Chairman of a combined Butterworth/Longman Group and there would still have been a worthwhile business for the Bond boys to go into if they wanted. Thanks to Maxwell and his phoney figures, it wasn't to be".

Millett claimed till the end that his mandate from Mr and Mrs Willis, on joining the Butterworth Board, was to find out why the profits were not better and do something about it. "There was never any question of the company being prepared for sale", he said many years later. But he had to "try to turn Butterworths into a viable entity". Five years later, this objective had metamorphosed into active negotiation with possble merger candidates in order to obtain a better return for shareholders and save the Company and staff from the embrace of Robert Maxwell, his distrust of whom was to be amply vindicated.

In a letter to the shareholders following the Maxwell offer, Millett said that they had three choices: Accept the Pergamon bid (which included a cash option); sell to someone else; or remain independent. He immediately set about activating counter-offers. He called the author (I was at the Frankfurt Book Fair) among no doubt others, with the message "Get your cheque book out".

A cash offer better than Maxwell's was received from a US corporation (Crowell Collier Macmillan), with whom Millett had parleyed in December 1966. However, doubts were expressed (not least by Robert Maxwell) about allowing Halsbury's Laws of England to be published by a foreign firm. The prospective takeover became a political issue and was mentioned by Harold Wilson in the House of Commons.

Millett's ace-in-the-hole was a large British corporation which already owned 10% of Butterworths' shares. As early as March 1964 Millett had talked with Don Rider, a Director of the International Publishing Corporation (IPC). Rider told him then that IPC would like to acquire a larger block of Butterworth shares "when the Bond boys come of age". So there was nothing sudden or inspirational about Millett's call on Cecil King, Chairman of IPC, to outbid Pergamon. The matter was resolved very quickly. Maxwell himself was not surprised at his defeat. In the light of his subsequent history as an arbitrageur, one wonders how many Butterworth shares he had bought before launching his bid. A Butterworth employee who had joined Pergamon just before the takeover struggle reported that Maxwell had been buying whatever Butterworth stock was available.

Ian Bond came home from Australia as soon as the Pergamon bid was intimated. Still estranged from his family, he put up at a friend's flat in London. Returning there late one night, he was accosted by two men who got out of a parked car and joined him at the door of the flat. "Mr Bond?" "Yes." "Of Butterworths?" "Yes." "You would have a very good job if you would consider Pergamon." With that, they turned away. Maxwell was obviously aware that Ian Bond was the hold-out of the Butterworth trustees.

As soon as the Pergamon bid was intimated, Millett set about gathering information to Maxwell's discredit. Several deeds of indemnity survive in the Butterworth files, including one protecting Millett from any suits brought by Maxwell. A Miss Kekwick was reported to be interviewing former Pergamon employees in search of derogatory information. Maxwell reported this to Seabrook Emery, who said he was shocked and would look into it. Several shareholders from whom nothing had been heard for years wrote to Butterworths expressing dissatisfaction with their dividends and demanding that the Pergamon offer be accepted.

However, discrediting Maxwell was not as easy then as it was to become twenty years later. The rapid growth of Pergamon and Maxwell's status as a Member of Parliament gave him a reasonably good reputation at that time. The fate of Butterworths became a personal battle between Millett and Maxwell. Butterworth staff in India and Australia were enlisted to seek evidence that Maxwell's recently hailed claims to have personally sold thousands of encyclopedias were false.

Ironically, Pergamon *minus* Maxwell would have been a good fit with Butterworths. Since being launched in 1951 with a small list of books and journals purchased from Butterworths, Pergamon had proved that it knew how to make a success of scientific publishing. It was Butterworths' weak area. An astute US publisher (Earl Coleman of Plenum) telephoned Millett from the Frankfurt Book Fair to offer £700,000 in cash for Butterworths' medical and scientific lists. Millett was not resistant to an American buyer.

Pergamon proved, in the end, to be the only enterprise that Maxwell personally developed and built. All his subsequent energies were more manipulative than creative. Pergamon was the product of his early years when his frenetic energy, charm, wiliness and financial acumen coincided with the post-war explosion of scientific research which provided the raw material for the fortunes of several successful scientific publishers - Springer in Germany; Elsevier in the Netherlands; Blackwell Scientific in the UK; or John Wiley in the US. By the 1960s, it was too late to ride the surge. Competition had become intense. Companies established in the 1950s were secure because they had strings of journals with devoted constituents. Pergamon, a product of the '50s, was sold to Elsevier for £400m in 1989. It remained the jewel in Maxwell's crown until he was forced to sell it to raise cash to cover his extravagant ambitions and ultimate malfeasance. Four years later, Elsevier merged with Reed International, bringing Butterworths and Pergamon into common ownership twenty-five years after the Maxwell/Millett struggle.

There was no synergy between Butterworths and IPC (as Reed was then known) in 1967. But by 1992 having Butterworths and Pergamon in their respective domains was one of the factors which brought Reed and Elsevier together.

Maxwell's three biographers record the part that Butterworths played in the Maxwell story, relating the catalytic effect that Maxwell had on Butterworths. Joe Haines, who was commissioned by Maxwell to write his biography, plays down the parts that Butterworths and Springer had played in Maxwell's early history as "little more than a small time experiment in partnership which had failed". The loss of his bids for Butterworths and for the *News of the World*, were "a severe disappointment to Maxwell", Haines relates, and were a prelude ("defeats ... made him even more keen and that keenness, in turn, made him incautious") to his disastrous romance with Saul Steinberg's Leasco in 1969.

Tom Bower, in *Maxwell The Outsider*, relating the Maxwell/Millett struggle, comments that "for the first time in Maxwell's career, a takeover battle became ferociously personal". Peter Thompson and Anthony Delano in *Maxwell, A Portrait of Power* described Millett as "one of the few people in London who seem prepared to act on the doubts he had about Maxwell's methods". The differing attitudes of the three biographies are reflected in their descriptions of the Maxwell defeat. "A multi-million pound offer for Butterworths was rejected" (Haines). "Maxwell reluctantly conceded defeat" (Bower). "Maxwell's boarding attempt was repelled" (Thompson/Delano).

The subsequent histories of Pergamon and Butterworths support Millett's belief that he "saved" Butterworths from Maxwell. Although Butterworths was not a good strategic fit with IPC, it was to flourish in its new corporate home to an extent that would make the shareholders subsequently reflect that the £7.5m paid by IPC was a bargain price. By 1985, Butterworths was making £20m a year in pre-tax profits. Maxwell stated to *Campaign*, the advertising newspaper that his bid for Butterworths had been unsuccessful "because IPC decided to pay two million more than I was offering and it turned out to be two million more than the business was worth".

During the short takeover battle, Ian Bond was fighting his own corner. He did not want the company to be sold, and felt that IPC offered only money and respectability. It had no knowledge or expertise in Butterworths' kind of publishing, and its unionised newspaper culture was remote from the sedate servitude of Butterworth employees. Longman, he felt, would have been a better choice, as a merger, not a takeover.

With the sale to IPC, Millett felt he had discharged his duties to the shareholders who voted unanimously for the IPC offer, with Mrs Willis and Ian's brother Brian signifying the acceptance of the Bond Trust.

Mrs Willis put the best face that she could on the takeover. Much was made of fending off Maxwell, the immigrant, and American suitors. On 2 November 1967, the date on which the sale to IPC was settled, Mrs Willis wrote to the Old Butterworthians:

> As the senior member of the Old Butterworthians, I am
> writing to you to express my deep sorrow which I am
> certain everyone of us shares, over the new era that has
> been sprung upon us, as with so many others and which
> was unavoidable. I am sure that all must realize that every
> possible effort has been made to do what was best for the
> company, its members both active and retired and the main
> body of shareholders. It seemed unthinkable that the Laws
> of England would be published by any other country, so it

is some consolation that the control remains in this country, that the name of Butterworth will continue, and that every consideration will be given to those who have, and are working for it. We can look back with pride that during these most difficult days the prestige of the Company both at home and overseas was held so high. Mr Bond would have been so proud. I just want [you] all to know that we have done our best and what we feel Mr Bond would have liked in these circumstances.

On the same date, Mrs Willis wrote to Cecil King:

I feel I must write to you a short note to wish you good luck and happiness with Butterworths.

It is a great firm and it has been much loved by the family through the years.

I felt you might like to know that it was taken over by my late husband, Stanley Bond, when he was seventeen with one man and a boy!

I am sure he would be proud to know that you have kept it in British hands, and will look after it and those who work in it, in the British way.

David Willis insisted on a clause in the sales agreement that Ian Bond would be guaranteed an appointment within the Mirror Group. Cecil King told Ian Bond that he had met his father "while fishing the River Dee before the war" and felt that Stanley Bond would have been very happy with the amalgamation. "It was surely the best deal that King made in his whole life", reflected Ian Bond twenty-five years later. He declined the job and went to work instead for Hambros Bank.

Deeply dissatisfied with the way he had been overruled, Ian Bond took legal advice from Norton Rose, who were then Hambros' lawyers. The Bond Family Trust was closely studied by these advisers, but they concluded that nothing could be done by way of redress without the support of Mrs Willis, who had a power of attorney which she could have used to frustrate any action that Ian might contemplate. Ian Bond believes that his mother, coming from an old aristocratic family, had an inbred suspicion of anyone who achieved commercial success. Presumably she had repressed this suspicion when she married Stanley Bond.

Millett and his merchant bank advisers recommended that Butterworths shareholders should sell their IPC shares immediately. On consummation of the sale, Millett resigned his chairmanship and his membership of the Butterworth Board; as did Emery and Niekirk. Twenty-five years after Bond's death a few who had joined Butterworths under his command were finally invited to participate in the shaping of the company which they had served for so long. Simon Partridge (law publisher), Sheila Carey (scientific) and David Perry (sales) were elected to the Board. Kay Jones was appointed Deputy Managing Director and Ian Dickson, the Financial Director hired by Millett from Penguin, was appointed Managing Director.

Usually, when a company is sold, it passes from a period of peace and stability into one of turmoil and change. With Butterworths, it was the other way round. After the turbulence of the Millett years, the corporate life seemed peaceful. The new owners did not know quite what they should do with Butterworths, the purchase of which had been a personal decision by Cecil King. King himself was about to be eclipsed when he tried to use the *Daily Mirror* to challenge the Labour Government. Before his departure, he developed a plan to form a diversified book division within IPC and had personally assumed chairmanship of the Butterworth Board.

The boss of the new book division was Paul Hamlyn, whose company IPC had also recently purchased. Hamlyn did not stay for long. He was essentially an entrepreneur, not a corporate man.

Born and nurtured under the autocracy of personal ownership; consigned for twenty years to the foster care of trustees and heirs who lacked the passion and vision of the founder, delivered by them into the control of a man who could perceive its weaknesses but not its strengths, Butterworths finally arrived, blinking with astonishment, into the world of public ownership, where the shareholder is king and performance is all. But Butterworths had become an institution, capable of satisfying the most demanding owners. It was to flourish, developing and modernizing the basic ideas of its founder, beyond his dream.

# Acknowledgements

I could not have written this book without the help of Ian Bond, who unlocked many mysteries and told me frankly his own story.

I am also grateful to the late Richard Millett with whom I had many conversations and much correspondence. While sensitive to his role as the catalyst of Butterworths in the 1960s, he was meticulous with information, making many phone calls to survivors from the period to check his memories.

I would also like to express my gratitude to Richard Millett Jr who checked the proofs.

A key witness to the story was Sir Peter Smithers who received me graciously at his home on the shore of Lake Como in Switzerland.

I also learned much from Barry Rose, a close in-house observer from the day he was appointed Editor of *The Justice of the Peace* at the age of nineteen.

I was not able to meet Myrtle Willis or her husband David. She was in many ways the enigmatic central figure in the story.

I owe an enormous debt to Kay Jones, who did monumental research into the Butterworth archives for the first edition of the company history.

Roger Hedley-Jones, Company Secretary during the years of my tenure was immensely helpful in spotting documents in the archives which helped to illuminate the story.

Among many kindnesses extended by Ian Bond was an interview with Stanley Bond's niece Marjory, who in her nineties retained graphic memories of her time with Uncle Stanley.

An especially nostalgic letter in the extensive correspondence aroused by the book was from Sir Alex Cairncross, whose famous textbook Stanley Bond had published by mistake – I had been in Sir Alex's class at Glasgow University in 1938.

I am indebted finally to my successor Neville Cusworth who commissioned me to write the book in 1990 and has been unfailingly supportive. In 1995 we agreed to shelve it in favour of the second edition of the company history. By the time this work was ready for publication Neville had retired and Butterworths were no longer interested in publishing it. After a talk I gave to the Butterworth pensioners, one of them suggested I approach John Sinkins of Wildy & Sons, a company even older than Butterworths. I am grateful to Brian Hill of Wildy's for his skill and patience in bringing the book to fruition.